What's You BACON?

Uncover Your 5 Sizzling Secrets of Business Success!

Master Happiness
With
Marty Jalove

Dedicated to

my Mother,
who demonstrated the benefits of great stories,

and to

my Father,
who told me to work with my brain, not my back.

Contents

Special Acknowledgements to

David Allen, Amazon, Maya Angelou, Apple, Ben & Jerry's, Blockbuster, Richard Branson, Francesco Cirillo, Coca-Cola, Jim Collins, Confucius, Steven M.R. Covey, Mihaly Csikszentmihalyi, James Cunningham, George Doran, Carol Dweck, Thomas A. Edison, President Dwight Eisenhower, Henry Ford, Mahatma Gandhi, Seth Godin, Google, Todd W. Hall, Harvard Business Review, Todd Henry, Hubspot, Albert Humphrey, Kristi Jalove, Joe Janicki, Jasper, Steve Jobs, Michael Jordan, Kodak, Joe Lazauskas, Jin Lazier, Kelly Leonard, McDonald's, Arthur Miller, Donald Miller, Jason Miller, Barbara Minto, Vilfredo Pareto, C. Northcote Parkinson, Ron Penner, Laura Ries, Antoine de Saint-Exupery, Shane Snow, Tesla, Brian Tracy, Sun Tzu, Virgin Group, Gino Wickman, Jeremy Wright, Yahoo, Tom Yorton, and the countless Coaches and many Mentors who have guided me throughout my life.

Introduction

Pork and Beans

My dad may not have said much, but the words he did share with me were pure gold. When I was just a kid, all I wanted was to connect with him, be like him, and earn his respect and admiration. I used to tag along with him during his home-construction projects, trying to be a worthwhile assistant. Whatever TV show he watched; I quickly made it my favorite too. But one of my fondest memories was watching my dad eat pork and beans right out of the can. For some reason, I thought that that was the coolest thing ever.

He shared those beans with me, and while eating them, I discovered something squishy in the sauce. Curious, I asked my dad what it was. He looked at me with a smile and said, "That, my son, is BACON - the true magic behind pork and beans."

Now, if you've ever had pork and beans, you know how challenging it is to find a piece of bacon among all those beans. It's like searching for a needle in a haystack! I always thought it should be called "Beans, Beans, Beans, and a Chance of Pork." But according to my dad, that little piece of bacon is all that's needed to make a can of beans truly special. Bacon is like a magical ingredient that enhances everything it touches. We can all be filled with beans, but it's up to each of us to uncover our own bacon. The thing that makes us truly special, different, and unique. And let me tell you, discovering your bacon is even more amazing than eating it.

As I grew older, my dad told me that it was fine to mimic and mirror others, but it's important to define our own paths of happiness. Sometimes it's okay to conform, but stepping outside the box, zigging while others zag, is our first step toward fulfilling our purpose.

Even to this day, I see some of my father in my actions and decisions. But I've learned to add my own twist. I still eat pork and beans, but I put them in my chili, I no longer eat them straight from the can (usually).

My dad's thoughts have stayed with me and continue to guide me in helping countless small businesses, teams, and individuals uncover their own bacon, their uniqueness, and their differentiation. I find joy in helping people uncover and capitalize on what makes them special and makes them smile.

So, my question to you is this:

"What's Your Bacon?"

Purpose of the Workbook

I've always been driven by an entrepreneurial spirit. At the heart of it all, I believe that staying true to myself and using my unique talents to help others is the key to genuine happiness. I'm a perpetual learner, constantly observing, reading, listening, and experimenting. Deep down, I have a burning desire to share everything I know with as many people as I can. I firmly believe in the principles of **Shine, Sharpen, and Share**.

Shining is about acknowledging my skills, talents, and gifts. It's not about claiming superiority, but about taking pride in who I am and who I aspire to be.

Sharpening represents my continuous pursuit of knowledge and improvement. It's about honing my skills and ensuring that every day is an opportunity for learning something new.

Sharing, as the term implies, is about giving. What's the point of having talents that I continually nurture and improve if I don't share them with others? Whether I sell, trade, or give away my knowledge, it's crucial that it doesn't go to waste.

The reason I wrote this book is because I embody these three principles—Shine, Sharpen, Share—I'm not only interested in carving out a successful path for myself, but also inspiring others to do the same. I hope that my belief system encourages everyone to recognize their strengths, commit to lifelong learning, and generously share their gifts with the world.

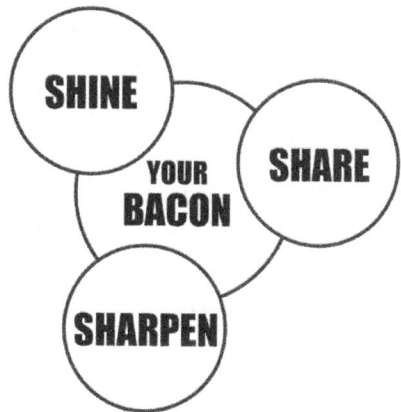

How to Use the Book

I have a passion for knowledge, yet lengthy, monotonous books are not my cup of tea. Therefore, this book is designed with smaller, digestible sections within each chapter. Feel free to peruse the book at your own pace, gleaning insights as you traverse. The book is structured into intros, extras, and activities, which I encourage you to engage with at your leisure. Revisit sections as required for reinforcement. I recommend beginning with the first chapter, but feel free to navigate freely through the book thereafter. My aspiration is for you to discover at least one valuable idea from each chapter—insights that you can implement straight away. I am confident that if you do so, this book will become a manual you return to as your business flourishes and transforms. I assure you; you'll uncover practical ideas and fresh strategies that will guide you in gaining clarity, feeling accomplished, and enjoying the journey.

Chewing the Fat

The section of this book called "Chewing the Fat" is about sharing a story that helps illustrate the message of that chapter. The stories are a little light-hearted because I believe that all work and no play is the surest way to waste your day.

The Appetizers

This section is for people who want to get through the reading and onto the implementing quickly. Here I present you with some tasty core ideas that are going to get your tummy growling for more. Use this section as a reminder of what you could be doing and should be doing. I encourage you to digest the appetizers and then come back later to chew on the rest of the book when you are ready to sizzle!

The Buffet

I aim to serve up a veritable feast of insights, more than you could possibly devour in one go. So, pull up a chair and browse through this smorgasbord of ideas and actionable steps to construct the enterprise you've always envisioned. In this banquet of knowledge, you'll gorge on the Why's, What's, and How's of your continuously evolving venture. You'll learn about the strategic steps to take, the effective tools to employ, and the compelling message to broadcast. So, ready your intellectual appetite and let's embark on this journey together. Bon appétit!

Time to OINK

This section of the book is filled with exercises and worksheets designed for both individual and team participation. These worksheets are your steppingstones to start you down the right path and can be repeatedly referred to and revised as often as needed.

O - Organize: The reason for these worksheets to help you in organizing your thoughts and understanding. These worksheets break down complex concepts into manageable tasks that you can tackle at your own pace.

I - Internalize: I believe that doing these worksheets will help you internalize what you've learned. By taking the time to complete these assignments, you're reinforcing the knowledge you've gained and making it stick.

N - Nurture: Completing these worksheets nurtures a sense of responsibility and discipline. It is proof to yourself that you are committed to evolving and succeeding. It encourages you to set time aside for the learning that will lead to earning.

K - Knowledge: The ultimate goal of these worksheets is the acquisition of knowledge. Every assignment completed expands your understanding and takes you one step closer to building your better business.

BLT is your Call to Action

B - Begin Immediately: As soon as you've gained new knowledge, put it into practice. The best way to solidify learning is through action. Don't wait for the "perfect" moment; start now.

L - Learn Continuously: Learning is an endless journey. Never stop seeking new information and challenging yourself. Remember, every experience offers a lesson.

T - Teach Others: Sharing your knowledge not only helps others but also reinforces what you've learned. Teaching invites you to fully understand a concept and see it from different perspectives.

I am deeply grateful that you have chosen to embark on this journey with me through the pages of this book. Your decision to invest your precious time in exploring the insights and wisdom within these chapters is truly humbling. Trusting me as the author to guide you on this path is an honour I don't take lightly. Let's dive into this together, ignite our entrepreneurial spirits, and uncover the keys to unlocking success. It's time to SIZZLE!

BELIEFS ARE YOUR BRAND

Beliefs, Values, Vision, and Mission: *Think of these as the secret recipe for your grandma's famous pie - unique, heartwarming, and irresistible. They are the ingredients that give your small business its distinct flavor and identity. They guide your decisions, shape your culture, and attract customers who share your values. Without them, you're just another pie in the bakery.*

"Your beliefs become your thoughts. Your thoughts become your words. Your words become your actions. Your actions become your habits. Your habits become your values. Your values become your destiny."

– M.K. Gandhi

Chewing the Fat

What's Your Bacon?

I used to dread Mondays. Whether it was school or my various jobs as an ambitious young dreamer, I would count down the days until the weekend and dread the thought of facing Monday mornings. Sometimes, the dislike for Mondays was so intense that it made me physically ill. I'm sure I'm not the only one who has felt this way. I found myself asking the same question again and again: what could make going to sleep on Sunday night impossible because I was so excited for Monday morning? What could I promise myself every morning that would make me want to sing and dance?

For me, the answer was BACON!

Bacon is that magical meat that can make anything and everything it touches a little bit better. That salty, savory treat became my inspiration to wake up every morning with a smile on my face. Of course, it's not practical to make a living by simply eating bacon every morning (trust me, I've tried). So instead of the BACON for chewing, I now concentrate on the B.A.C.O.N. for doing! BACON is the many acronyms that I live by and use to teach others.

B - Believe in yourself,
A - Anticipate obstacles,
C - Confront your fears by
O - Observing and learning and
N - Nudge other people to do the same thing!

Now here's my question for you:
"What's Your Bacon?"

The Appetizers

The Power of Beliefs - How Your Values Shape Your Personal and Professional Brand

Our beliefs are more than just opinions or thoughts; they are the foundation of our personal and professional brand. Beliefs reflect our core values and our vision for the future. When we clarify our beliefs, we are better equipped to create a shortlist of our values that reflect the way we see ourselves and how we want others to perceive us. When we live according to our beliefs, we attract like-minded individuals and businesses that align with our values, making it easier to reach our goals and achieve success.

Understanding Your Beliefs

To define your beliefs, start by asking yourself a few fundamental questions: What is important to me? What do I believe in and stand for? Take the time to reflect and identify what is at the core of your being. Once you have defined your beliefs, write them down in a concise and clear way.

The Connection to Your Personal and Professional Brand

Your beliefs make up a significant part of your personal and professional brand. By living according to your beliefs, you create a consistent and authentic brand that people can connect with and trust. For instance, if one of your beliefs is to always deliver exceptional customer service, you can use this as a tool to build your brand, sell your products or services, and attract customers who share your values.

Making Decisions Based on Your Beliefs

Once you have identified your beliefs, making decisions becomes a lot easier. You can apply your beliefs to everything from hiring employees to developing your advertising strategy. By being clear on what is important to you, you are less likely to make decisions that are not aligned with your values. This allows you to stay true to yourself and your brand.

Walking Away from Business That Does Not Align with Your Beliefs

As entrepreneurs, it is natural to want to take on every opportunity and grow your business as fast as possible. However, if a potential client or business opportunity does not align with your beliefs, it is important to walk away. Doing business with individuals or companies that do not share your values can hurt your brand and reputation in the long-term.

Impacts of Living According to Your Beliefs

One of the most significant impacts of living according to your beliefs is a sense of fulfillment and satisfaction. There is a sense of peace and clarity that comes from living your truth. When you align your actions with your beliefs, you increase your self-confidence and become a more authentic version of yourself. This, in turn, attracts life opportunities and business collaborations that are in keeping with your values.

Your beliefs are the cornerstone of your personal and professional brand. They shape your vision for the future, help you make decisions, and attract like-minded individuals to support your journey. By living according to your beliefs, you build a strong, authentic brand that people can trust and connect with. Remember to take the time to reflect on what is meaningful to you, and then use your beliefs to guide your actions and decisions. By doing so, you will create a fulfilling life and business that aligns with your values.

The Buffet

When it comes to building a successful business, both core beliefs and core values play integral roles, yet they serve different functions.

Core Beliefs in a business context are the fundamental assumptions or principles that the business is built upon. They underpin your business model and strategy, shaping the way you view your market, customers, competitors, and your own company. For example, a core belief could be "Our customers value quality over quantity" or "Innovation drives growth". These beliefs influence how you approach your business, make decisions, and define your success.

Core Values, on the other hand, are the guiding principles that dictate behavior and action within the business. They are the ethos of your company culture, driving how you conduct business, treat your employees, and serve your customers. Core values might include integrity, teamwork, customer service, or innovation. They help you establish a strong company culture and brand identity, guide your business decisions, and attract like-minded employees and customers.

So, while core beliefs shape your business strategy and your perception of the business landscape, core values guide the behaviors, ethics, and culture within your business. Both are crucial for building a business that is not only successful but also resilient, adaptable, and respected.

The 5 Core Values of Master Happiness, LLC

1. **Happiness:** My company thrives on mutual joy. I seek to foster relationships where shared happiness propels us to do our best work. I strive to cultivate this joy within our teams, believing that "Happy employees attract happy customers, and happy customers come back with friends."

2. **Inspiration:** I look for energy sharers and growth seekers. I only work with those who want to inspire each other to collectively reach new heights. Embracing challenges from my clients, we uncover solutions together. When we share the thrill of achieving a common goal, we believe nothing is unattainable.

3. **Creativity:** As an artist, writer, inventor, and lifelong learner, I am devoted to presenting my clients with truly innovative solutions. These out-of-the-box strategies emphasize their uniqueness and give them a competitive edge. Our discovery journey always begins with "What if", "Why not?", and "Yes, and!"

4. **Empathy:** I champion understanding. Through constant inquiry, I aim to intimately comprehend my clients and their customers' needs, helping us facilitate win-win scenarios. We will continuously learn and share experiences across industries. By empathizing with your needs, we can help find your solutions.

5. **Integrity:** Honesty forms the bedrock of our interactions. I respect the struggles you share with me, treating them as our secrets. I ensure our clients can trust me, knowing I'll always provide honest feedback—even if it means acknowledging that I may not be the right partner for them. I prefer to part ways than convince someone to work with me when we're not the right fit.

Uncover your true purpose in one sentence.

When building a successful business, both the vision statement and mission statement play crucial roles, but they serve different purposes.

Vision Statement is your business's long-term goal or where you see your company in the future. It's aspirational, providing a clear idea of what the company aims to achieve in the long run. It serves as a guidepost for where the business is headed and provides inspiration and direction.

Here are four vision statements from successful companies:

1. **Amazon:** "Our vision is to be earth's most customer-centric company; to build a place where people can come to find and discover anything they might want to buy online."

2. **Ben & Jerry's:** "Making the best ice cream in the nicest possible way."

3. **Apple:** "To make the best products on earth and to leave the world better than we found it."

4. **Master Happiness:** "To be a driving force in helping all people find their sizzle and uncover their own paths of happiness."

A Mission Statement explains the purpose of your business, outlining why it exists and what it does to achieve its vision. It's more focused on the present and details the practical tactics your company will use. It's more about the 'how' of your operations. In essence, while a vision statement outlines the future state your business aspires to reach, a mission statement describes the current approach your business will take to achieve that future state. Both are vital in providing direction, setting goals, making decisions, and shaping strategy.

Here are four mission statements from successful companies:

1. **Coca-Cola:** "To refresh the world...to inspire moments of optimism and happiness...to create value and make a difference."

2. **Google:** "To organize the world's information and make it universally accessible and useful.

3. **Tesla:** "To accelerate the world's transition to sustainable energy."

4. **Master Happiness:** "To help small-businesses, teams, and individuals find focus, feel fulfilled, and have fun."

Time to Oink!
Organize, Internalize, and Nurture the Knowledge!

Activity #1 – Your Venn Diagram

Believe in yourself before expecting others to believe in you. We often hear the phrase "You are special, unique, and necessary" so frequently that its true meaning gets lost. But it's crucial to recognize our own worth. Take the time to acknowledge what you excel at and make a list of your greatest strengths. It doesn't mean you have to be the best in the world at these things, but rather that you possess qualities, skills, and talents that are worth celebrating.

What truly makes you amazing is not just one or two talents, but the beautiful combination and growth of your incredible abilities and gifts. Embrace your brilliance without hesitation. Go ahead and showcase your talents, just remember to do so without diminishing others.

Let's kickstart this process by jotting down a short list of some of the things that you're good at and things that bring you joy. Revel in your greatness and embrace your awesomeness!

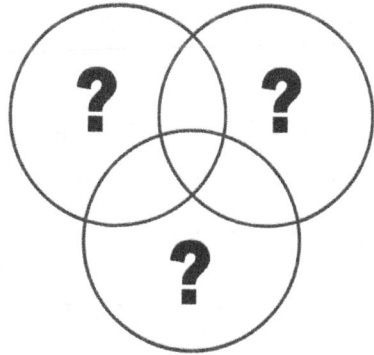

Write these talents in a group of intersecting circles and create a Venn Diagram of your amazing self. Maybe you excel in Excel, love exploring caves, reeling in Marlin, and just learned the language of Venezuela. You may not be the world's greatest at any one of these things, but you just may be the World's Greatest Spanish Speaking, Spreadsheeting, Sportfishing, Spelunker! So, Congratulations, that is something to be proud of and worth believing in!

Activity #2 - Your Core Values

What are the guiding principles that define your company? Just as Gandhi said, your beliefs lead to your values which lead to your destiny. These core values are the essence of who you are and what you stand for. They will shape your brand and be the foundation on which you build your success. These values should be so important to you that you would rather lose a client or close your doors than compromise them.

At first, it may seem like an overwhelming task. But once you uncover your core values, everything else will fall into place. It's the key to answering other questions and resolving issues with ease.

1. Start by unleashing your creativity. List all the things that you believe in - without holding back. List the words and phrases that you stand for, that define you, and how you want your company to be viewed. Whether it's 20 or even 100 words, terms, or phrases, let them flow. Be true to yourself and write with integrity and honesty. These values reflect who you are and what your business stands for.

2. Take a break for a couple of days and come back with fresh eyes. Identify the values that truly resonate with you. Combine and define them to create a short list of 5 to 7 essential values. Compressing your values to a short list will ensure that they are truly meaningful, and they represent who you are, who you want to be, and how you want to be viewed.

3. Step away again for a few days. Revisit your lists, both the current and the original. Are these the values you want to proudly share with the world? Do they truly represent the essence of your company?

4. Involve your partners or team in this enlightening exercise. Ask them to embark on the same journey independently. When you come together, compare your lists. Each person should explain why they chose the values they did and what they mean to them.

5. It's time to finalize your list. Condense your list to no more than seven Core Values of just one or two words each. This simplicity will make them more compelling and impactful when shared.

6. Now write one sentence for each of your core values. This should explain your definition of each value, what they mean to you, and how they reflect your company.

7. Print this out, hang it on your wall, add it to your website, and proudly share it with your employees and customers.

Embrace this journey of self-discovery and honesty. Uncover your core values and see how aligned you and your team truly are. It's a powerful exercise that will set you on the path to success. Here's a list of 25 powerful core value examples to ignite your creativity and push you towards success. Don't stop at this list – let your imagination run wild and wander as you create your own list.

Accountability

Adaptability

Agility

Authenticity

Collaboration

Continuous improvement

Customer-focused

Efficiency

Empowerment

Excellence

Fairness

Flexibility

Honesty

Humility

Innovation

Passion

Patience

Quality

Respect

Results-driven.

Social responsibility

Teamwork

Transparency

Trust

Work-life balance

Activity #3 - Crafting a Vision Statement

A company vision statement is a critical element in setting the tone and direction of your organization. It helps to define your aspirations, values, and direction. Just as creating a core value list is essential, crafting a vision statement is equally important. An excellent vision statement is comprehensive, inspiring, and forward-thinking. However, creating one can be challenging. Here are five easy steps to follow that will help you create a powerful vision statement for your company now that you have laid out your core values.

Brainstorming Session with Your Team

The first step to crafting a vision statement is to hold a brainstorming session with your team. Start by reviewing your list of core values, and then engage your team to discuss the direction they believe your company should take. Encourage open and honest communication and give every member a chance to share their ideas.

During this session, capture the ideas on a flip chart or whiteboard. Ensure you listen carefully to everyone and look for common themes. Use those themes as a foundation to create a meaningful and purposeful vision statement.

Define the Time Frame

A good vision statement should be set for the long term, but it should have a time frame. Define the time frame based on your company's business model, your industry, and where you see your organization in the future. Decide if you want to set up a five, ten, or fifteen-year vision. The timeline you choose should be realistic and achievable.

Make it Simple and Memorable

A memorable vision statement should be short, memorable, and easy to understand. Use plain language and make it simple for your staff to internalize. Avoid using jargon or buzzwords that may confuse your team. The more straightforward your vision statement is, the easier it is for employees to understand and relate to it.

Align it with Your Core Values

Your company's core values are the foundation of your organization. Your vision statement should align with your core values and resonate with your employees. Ensure that the words of your vision statement are consistent with your core values' tone and language.

Refer to your core values list and ensure that your vision statement is consistent with each of them. If you don't have any core values yet, establish them first before crafting your vision statement.

Get Feedback and Revise as Needed

Once you have created a draft of your vision statement, share it with your team and stakeholders. Get feedback on whether the statement represents your team's aspirations and vision. Ensure your vision statement resonates with all stakeholders, including your customers, employees, investors, and partners.

Get feedback from your Business Coach and Mentors. These fresh eyes will add a different perspective and force you to explain your thoughts. Use this feedback to refine your vision statement. Continue to revise it until it reflects the direction, values, and aspirations of your entire organization.

Your company's vision statement is critical in giving your team direction, purpose, and focus. It guides your organization's growth, inspires your workforce, and sets the tone for your company culture. Crafting a powerful vision statement is not a one-time event; it's an ongoing process. By following the simple five steps above, you can create a clear and inspiring vision statement that aligns with your organization's core values. Remember, your vision statement should be simple, concise, inspiring, and impactful. Don't be afraid to revise it as your company evolves, and you achieve your goals.

Activity #4 - Crafting a Mission Statement

It's no secret that businesses that have a clear understanding of their vision, values, and mission thrive and produce better results. That's why creating a mission statement is an essential part of strategic planning for any company. A mission statement helps to define the company's direction and its purpose. Once you've identified your company's core values and vision statement, it's time to craft a mission statement. Follow these five in creating a mission statement that resonates with your company's culture and brand.

Define Your Company's Purpose

Your mission statement should capture the fundamental reason why your company exists. Look at your vision statement and core values and use them as a baseline for defining your company's purpose. Ask yourself, what problem does your company solve for its customers? What are your company's strengths and unique selling points? Your mission statement should reflect these qualities.

Keep It Short and Simple

When crafting your mission statement, remember that less is more. Keep it short and straightforward, so that it's easy to remember and communicate. Generally, a mission statement should be no longer than two sentences. A concise, well-crafted mission statement will be easier to remember and communicate to your employees, customers, and stakeholders.

Make It Unique

Your mission statement should be unique to your business and capture your brand's personality. Avoid generic, vague statements that could apply to any business. For example, "we strive to provide the best customer service." While this may be a noble goal, it's something that every other business is trying to achieve. Instead, use your unique selling points to guide your mission statement. What makes your business stand out from the crowd?

Keep It Action-Oriented

Your mission statement should be actionable and inspire action in your employees and customers. Use strong, active verbs that convey a sense of purpose and urgency. For example, "We empower people to achieve their goals through innovative technology." This statement not only defines your company's purpose but also communicates the action that you want your customers to take.

Get Feedback from Your Team

Your employees are the backbone of your business, and their input and feedback are valuable in crafting a mission statement that accurately reflects your company's values and purpose. Gather input from your team and encourage them to share their thoughts and ideas. This will not only result in a more accurate mission statement but also a stronger sense of team unity.

Creating a mission statement is an important step in defining your company's direction and purpose. A well-crafted mission statement should be unique to your brand, actionable, and memorable. By following these five steps, you can create a mission statement that accurately reflects your company's values, inspires action, and motivates your team to achieve your goals. Remember, your mission statement should be a guiding principle that shapes your company's culture and direction for years to come.

Activity #5 - Dreams and Goals

As a small-business owner, you probably have a lot of aspirations and good intentions for your company. Maybe you want to increase revenue, expand your product line, or improve employee morale. However, without a plan, these ideas may just remain dreams. That's why it's important to write down your goals and create a strategy for achieving them. Create SMART goals – a tool developed by George Doran, Arthur Miller, and James Cunningham that will help you craft specific, measurable, attainable, realistic, and timely goals for your business.

S – Specific. The first step in creating a SMART goal is to make it specific. This means that your goal should be clear and detailed, so everyone involved knows exactly what you're aiming for. For example, instead of saying "we want to increase sales," a specific goal would be "we want to increase sales by 10% in the next quarter by focusing on our social media marketing strategy."

M – Measurable. The next step is to make your goal measurable, meaning you need to come up with a way to track your progress. For example, if your goal is to increase sales, you could measure it by tracking the number of new customers, the total revenue generated, or the number of items sold. By setting measurable goals, you can see how well you're progressing and adjust your strategy as needed.

A – Attainable. While it's important to set ambitious goals, they also need to be attainable. It's great to aim for the stars, but if your goal is completely unrealistic, you're setting yourself up for failure. When setting goals, consider your resources, your team's capabilities, and any external factors that might impact your ability to achieve the goal.

R – Realistic. In addition to being attainable, your goal also needs to be realistic. This means that it should align with your company's values, mission, and overall strategy. If your goal doesn't make sense for your business, it's unlikely that you'll be able to achieve it. A realistic goal is one that's challenging but still within reach.

T – Timely. The final step in creating a SMART goal is to make it timely, which means setting a deadline for achieving the goal. Without a deadline, it's easy to put things off and never make any progress. By setting a specific timeframe, you can stay focused on what needs to be done and ensure that you're making progress towards your goal.

Setting goals is essential for small-business owners who want to grow and succeed. However, just having a goal isn't enough – you need to create a plan for achieving it. By using the SMART goals framework, you can create specific, measurable, attainable, realistic, and timely goals that will help you take your business to the next level. So, take some time to reflect on your goals, write them down, and develop a SMART action plan to achieve them. You'll be amazed at how much progress you can make when you have a clear vision and a roadmap for success.

So How Do You Start Achieving Your Ultimate Business Goals?

Setting goals can seem like a daunting task, especially when it comes to achieving long-term business goals. As a small-business owner, it's important to have a clear vision and plan in place to help you reach your Ultimate Goal. I feel that the best way to start setting and achieving your long-term business goals by breaking them down into actionable steps. No matter how big or small your business may be, this approach can work wonders in helping you achieve your dreams.

1. Start by dreaming big! Write down the craziest, most unimaginable, and almost impossible goals for your business. Let your mind run wild and be playful in creating this vision. This is a great opportunity to let yourself free-think and brainstorm as a visionary. Once you have these ideas, it's now time to take a few days to reflect and come up with your realistic, long-term goals for your business. This could include anything from retiring to franchising your business.
2. After you have your long-term goal, start writing a list of all the things you need to accomplish in the next 10 years to make your ultimate dreams come true. This process will help you envision the path you need to take to achieve your ultimate goal.
3. Next, ask yourself what you need to accomplish in the next 3 years to hit your 10-year goal. This approach allows you to break down your long-term goal into more manageable and achievable milestones.
4. Now, take the goals you've identified for the next 3 years and ask yourself what you need to accomplish this year to realize those goals. This step will help you focus on what's truly important in the short-term and prioritize your efforts accordingly.
5. Finally, break down your goals into quarterly and monthly targets. Ask yourself what you need to get done right now to hit your 1-year goals. Be specific and set realistic targets for yourself.

Setting and achieving long-term business goals requires focus, dedication, and a plan of action. By breaking down your Ultimate Goals into manageable steps, you can make steady progress over time and ultimately achieve your dreams. Remember, your goals are not set in stone, so don't be afraid to make necessary adjustments along the way. Involve your team in this process and help them set their own goals, and watch as you all succeed together. With a clear plan, vision, and the right mindset, you can start achieving your ultimate business goals today!

Download the Worksheets

Worksheet: Find your Passion
Worksheet: Find your Mission
Worksheet: Values and Vision
Worksheet: Setting Goals

BLT

Begin Immediately, Learn Continuously, and Teach Others!

It's time to get cooking! Fire up that entrepreneurial spirit and take the first sizzling steps towards greatness. It's time to grab your pen and get your thoughts and dreams down on paper.

Don't wait for tomorrow—start writing down your beliefs, values, vision, and mission right now. Let the savory aroma of success fill every corner of your business, enticing customers and setting you apart from the competition.

Remember, your business will evolve and improve as you nurture and refine your purpose and your goals. So, buckle up, jump in, and start your amazing journey!

I'm here, cheering you on from the sidelines, ready to provide that extra sprinkle of inspiration whenever you need it. Now, go forth and create a success story that will leave everyone craving for more!

ANALYTICS & ADAPTABILITY

Analytics and Processes: These are the unsung heroes, much like the stagehands in a theater production. Behind the scenes, they keep everything running smoothly. They help you measure performance, streamline operations, and make informed decisions. Without them, your small business could turn into a Shakespearean tragedy!

Being busy does not always mean real work. The object of all work is production or accomplishment and to either of these ends there must be forethought, system, planning, intelligence, and honest purpose, as well as perspiration. Seeming to do is not doing.

- Thomas A. Edison

Chewing the Fat

The Brotherhood of the Traveling Pints

A few years ago, my neighbors and I gathered in my backyard for a fun evening of laughter, drinks, and tossing wood into a fire. It was during this gathering that Andy casually mentioned his desire to build a bar in his backyard. Half-jokingly, he invited us to bring any scrap wood we had and bring it to his house the next day so we could see what we could create.

We laughed at the idea of having some careless construction as a permanent fixture in our yards. But then I had a thought: what if we made the bar mobile by adding wheels to it?

And so, the Brotherhood of the Traveling Pints and the legend of the Rolling Bars was born.

We began planning and dreaming. We set some simple rules for building these bars: no spending money, we could only use leftover lumber, scavenged screws, and other discarded items. The bars had to have a sturdy-ish top for gathering around and wheels for easy transportation. And that was it! A simple set of rules that we all understand and follow.

Our first bar was created from an old office tabletop, moving dollies, and pallets. We added a stair-rail footrest and tiki torches for decoration. Inside, there's an old kitchen cabinet, a wine-rack, and some unwanted bottles of spirits.

Since then, we've built bars using a toboggan and a wheelchair, an old workbench, a playground set, and even a golf bar with an umbrella that rolls on jogging-stroller wheels. But all following the same guidelines.

What started as a joke has brought families together. It's not just about the bars themselves, but the bonding that happens during the building process and the gatherings we have around them.

Each bar we create improves upon the last. We learn from our mistakes and focus on better design. We reflect on our first bar and can now identify all the things we could have done differently. But we learn from those experiences, adapt to available materials, and implement processes to make the next build easier and more enjoyable.

Building a Rolling Bar is like implementing business processes. You need a feasible plan, resources, and dedicated employees. Only then can you successfully build a Rolling Bar or create a thriving business that aligns current operations with desired outcomes.

The Appetizers

The Art of Analyzing and Adapting Your Processes

As we continue to navigate the ever-evolving landscape of business today, one thing is clear- the ability to analyze and adapt our processes is more important than ever. To remain competitive, efficient, and effective as an organization, we must constantly strive to improve our workflows across all departments. This means creating, reviewing, and rebuilding our processes to ensure we are maximizing our resources and achieving our goals. So, what does this process look like, and how can you get started? Let's get going.

Creating a Baseline: The first step in analyzing and adapting our processes is creating a baseline. This means taking a deep dive into all areas of the organization, including finance, customer success, management, strategy, quality, sales, marketing, and HR, to assess where we currently stand. What are our current workflows, goals, and challenges? By doing so, we can create a snapshot of where we are, and what areas need the most attention.

Prioritizing Needs: Once you have a baseline, it's time to prioritize the areas in which adapting processes will have the greatest impact. This means analyzing data, speaking with team members, and identifying the bottlenecks that are most affecting our efficiency. Once you have identified these bottlenecks, it's time to create a plan of action to address them.

Updating and Adapting: With a plan in place, it's time to start updating and adapting our processes. This may involve automating workflows, changing the way tasks are assigned, or rethinking how teams are structured. As you make these changes, it's important to keep an open line of communication with your team. Be transparent about why changes are being made and how they will impact their work.

Short-Term and Long-Term Goals: As you analyze and adapt your processes, it's important to keep both short-term and long-term goals in mind. Some changes may take longer to implement but will ultimately have a greater impact on the organization. As you make these changes, continue to monitor progress, and assess their effectiveness. Celebrate the small wins and use them as motivation to keep pushing forward.

The Importance of Continuous Analysis and Adaptation: Finally, it's important to recognize that analyzing and adapting our processes is not a one-time event. As business continues to evolve, our workflows will need to evolve as well. Make a commitment to continuous analysis and adaptation to remain agile and responsive as an organization.

Analyzing and adapting our processes can seem daunting, but it's an essential part of remaining competitive and effective in today's business environment. By creating a baseline, prioritizing needs, updating, and adapting, setting short-term and long-term goals, and committing to continuous improvement, we can empower our teams and drive success across the organization. Remember, this process is ongoing and requires commitment from all levels of the organization. Let's take a proactive approach to analyzing and adapting our processes to remain ahead of the curve.

Take a closer look at your business.

Automating, delegating, sub-contracting, or using a VA for certain processes can significantly increase efficiency and productivity in a small business. Here are some of the processes that every small business should consider reviewing:

Email Marketing: Email marketing automation can help businesses send out timely, personalized emails to customers based on their behavior or preferences. This can increase engagement, conversion rates, and customer loyalty.

Social Media Posting: Automating or sub-contracting social media posts can ensure consistency and save time. Businesses can schedule posts in advance for optimal times and maintain a regular presence on their chosen platforms. Many small businesses will find it beneficial to use an outside source that specializes in social media to run their campaigns.

Customer Relationship Management (CRM): As you grow, you will discover that CRM systems can automate the process of tracking customer interactions. This can better help you understand customer behavior and preferences, improve customer service, and identify sales opportunities.

Appointment Scheduling: Online appointment scheduling allows customers to book appointments at their convenience, reduces the chances of double-booking, and can send automated reminders to reduce no-shows. Beware: Don't allow these apps and programs to take away from your company's personal touch. Many customers still want to talk to another human being.

Customer Support: Using chatbots for customer support can provide instant responses to common customer queries, improving customer satisfaction and freeing up time for support staff to handle more complex issues. But let me remind you, these chatbots should assist you, not replace real people.

Lead Generation: There are many companies and automation tools that specialize in capturing leads. Use these sources for setting up initial meeting and answering basic questions. They will help you sort pull quality leads form a plethora of prospects and help improve conversion rates.

By automating these processes, small businesses can save time, reduce errors, improve customer service, and focus more on strategic, revenue-generating activities.

The Buffet

Importance of Business Analytics

For young entrepreneurs and those contemplating starting their own business, understanding the importance of Business Analytics is crucial. This process involves collecting, sorting, studying, and synthesizing your business's data to gain insights, make informed decisions, and strategize effectively.

Let's look at Streaming Services as an example. Their success is largely due to its use of analytics. They leveraged this tool to understand viewer preferences - what they watch, how long they watch it, when they pause or stop - and used these insights to create successful original content. By studying user behavior and feedback, streaming services can provide more of what their customers want, ultimately leading to increased customer satisfaction and growth.

In contrast, Blockbuster, once a giant in the video rental industry, neglected the power of analytics and failed to adapt to changing consumer demands and technological advancements. Despite the clear shift towards online streaming, Blockbuster continued to focus on their brick-and-mortar stores. This ill-informed decision, rooted in the lack of proper analysis of market trends and consumer behavior, led to the company's downfall.

Data-Driven Decisions: Business Analytics allows you to make decisions based on data, not assumptions. Whether it's deciding on a new product launch, identifying which marketing strategy works best, or determining optimal pricing, data can provide the insights you need.

Understand Your Customers: Analytics can help you better understand your customers' behaviors, needs, and preferences. This understanding can inform everything from product development to marketing strategy, helping you meet customer needs and build stronger relationships.

Identify Trends and Opportunities: Through analyzing market data, you can identify emerging trends, anticipate changes, and uncover new opportunities. This can give you a competitive edge and help you stay ahead of the game.

Improve Efficiency and Profitability: Business Analytics can also help you streamline operations, improve efficiency, and increase profitability. By identifying inefficiencies in your processes, you can implement solutions to save time and resources.

Risk Management: Predictive analytics can forecast potential risks and challenges, allowing you to develop contingency plans and mitigate risk.

Business Analytics is not just a buzzword; it's an essential tool for any entrepreneur. By leveraging data, you can make informed decisions, understand your customers, identify opportunities, improve efficiency, and manage risks, leading to sustainable growth and success for your business.

Understanding Your Business Processes

Business processes are the series of steps that your company takes to deliver a product or service to your customers. They can range from how you handle customer inquiries, to how you manufacture your products, to how you market your services. Understanding these processes is key to running an efficient and successful business.

Let's take McDonald's as an example. One of their key business processes is their food preparation system. They've perfected this process to ensure fast service without compromising on quality. Every step, from cooking the burgers to assembling the meals, is meticulously planned, and executed. This allows McDonald's to serve their customers quickly, which is a major part of their brand promise.

On the other hand, Kodak is an example of what can happen when a company fails to understand and adapt its business processes. Despite being a pioneer in the photography industry, Kodak was slow to adapt to the digital revolution. They stuck to their traditional film-based processes for too long, and by the time they tried to catch up, it was too late. The company filed for bankruptcy in 2012.

Efficiency: By understanding your business processes, you can identify inefficiencies and areas for improvement. This can help you save time and resources, increase productivity, and ultimately, boost your bottom line.

Quality Control: A thorough understanding of your business processes is essential for maintaining quality. It allows you to monitor each step of your operations and ensure that the final product or service meets your standards.

Scalability: If you plan to grow your business, you need to have scalable processes in place. Understanding your business processes allows you to plan for growth and ensure that your operations can handle increased demand.

Innovation: By understanding your business processes, you can identify opportunities for innovation. This could be anything from introducing new technology to streamline operations, to finding new ways to deliver your products or services.

Competitive Advantage: Finally, well-defined, and efficient business processes can give you a competitive edge. They can help you deliver better products or services, provide superior customer service, and operate more efficiently than your competitors.

Understanding your business processes is not just about knowing what happens in your business. It's about understanding how things happen, why they happen that way, and how they can be improved. It's about constantly seeking ways to do things better, faster, and more efficiently. And most importantly, it's about delivering value to your customers.

Staying Focused: Tips and Techniques:

Maintaining focus is crucial for productivity and success. Techniques like time-blocking, prioritizing tasks, and minimizing distractions can help.

Apple, under Steve Jobs' leadership, exemplified focus by streamlining product lines to concentrate on quality and innovation. Conversely, Yahoo failed to maintain focus, spreading itself too thin across multiple products and services, eventually losing its market position.

Staying focused is crucial for young entrepreneurs and those contemplating starting their own business for several reasons:

Prioritization: Starting a business involves juggling multiple tasks at once, from product development and marketing to sales and customer service. Maintaining focus allows entrepreneurs to prioritize tasks effectively, ensuring that the most critical aspects of the business are attended to first.

Efficiency: With focus, entrepreneurs can dedicate their energy to completing tasks thoroughly and efficiently, rather than spreading themselves thin across too many tasks and potentially compromising on quality.

Goal Achievement: Clear focus helps entrepreneurs set specific, measurable, achievable, relevant, and time-bound (SMART) goals. Staying focused on these goals and consistently working towards them increases the likelihood of achieving them.

Resilience: The journey of entrepreneurship is filled with challenges and setbacks. Staying focused on the end goal can help entrepreneurs navigate these obstacles and remain resilient in the face of adversity.

Decision Making: A focused entrepreneur can make better decisions because they have a clear vision of what they want to achieve. This clarity can guide their decision-making process, helping them make choices aligned with their business goals.

Resource Management: Focus enables entrepreneurs to manage their resources more effectively. It ensures that time, money, and effort are spent on areas that align with the business's strategic objectives and offer the highest return on investment.

Growth: By staying focused, entrepreneurs can identify opportunities for growth and expansion. They can concentrate on nurturing key areas of the business that drive growth, such as product innovation, market research, or customer relationship management.

In essence, focus is the compass that guides entrepreneurs through the complex journey of building a business. It illuminates the path, helping them navigate challenges, make informed decisions, manage resources, and ultimately, achieve their business goals.

Delegating Effectively - When and How

As an entrepreneur, you wear many hats. You're the strategist, the marketer, the salesperson, the customer service rep, and the list goes on and on. But as your business grows, you'll find that you can't (and shouldn't) do everything yourself. This is where effective delegation comes in.

Delegation is the process of assigning tasks or responsibilities to others, allowing you to focus on strategic tasks that require your expertise. It's about recognizing the strengths of your team members and empowering them to take ownership of certain tasks or projects.

Richard Branson, the founder of Virgin Group, is a great example of an effective delegator. He attributes much of his success to delegation, stating that it has allowed him to focus on the bigger picture and build multiple successful businesses.

So, how can young entrepreneurs delegate effectively? Here are some tips:

Identify Tasks to Delegate: Not all tasks should be delegated. Start by identifying tasks that can be effectively completed by others. These might be tasks that are time-consuming, outside your area of expertise, or not critical to your core business goals.

Choose the Right Person: Delegate tasks to people who have the skills and knowledge to complete them effectively. Consider their workload, skills, experience, and interest in the task.

Communicate Clearly: When delegating, clearly communicate the task, expectations, deadlines, and any necessary information. Ensure the person understands the task and feels comfortable asking questions.

Empower and Trust: Delegation involves trust. Empower your team members by giving them the autonomy to complete tasks in their own way. Trust that they will do a good job.

Monitor Progress and Give Feedback: Check in periodically to monitor progress, offer assistance, and provide feedback. However, avoid micromanaging as it can undermine trust and empowerment.

Recognize and Reward: Acknowledge the efforts and achievements of your team members. Recognition and rewards can boost morale and motivate your team.

Delegation is a crucial skill for entrepreneurs. It not only helps you manage your workload but also empowers your team, fosters trust, and drives your business towards success. As Richard Branson said, "If you really want to grow as an entrepreneur, you've got to learn to delegate."

Automation - Tools and Strategies

In our fast-paced digital world, automation has become a powerful tool for businesses, big and small. It's about using technology to automate repetitive tasks, thereby improving efficiency, reducing errors, and freeing up time for more strategic tasks.

Take Amazon, for example. They use automation extensively in their warehouses through robots that retrieve items, helping to improve efficiency, accuracy, and speed. This has allowed Amazon to handle a vast number of orders quickly and accurately, contributing significantly to their success.

However, automation is not without its pitfalls. Knight Capital Group, a financial services firm, provides a cautionary tale. In 2012, they implemented a new automated software that had a glitch, leading to a staggering $440 million trading loss in just 45 minutes.

So, how can young entrepreneurs implement automation effectively in their businesses? Here are some steps:

Identify Repetitive Tasks: Start by identifying tasks that are repetitive and don't require much human judgment. These could include scheduling social media posts, sending reminder emails, or generating invoices.

Choose the Right Tools: There are many automation tools available, each designed for different tasks. Do your research to find the ones that best suit your needs. Such as QuickBooks for accounting.

Plan and Test: Before fully implementing an automation tool, plan out how it will fit into your current processes. Test the tool thoroughly to ensure it works as expected and train your team on how to use it.

Monitor and Adjust: Even after you've implemented automation, it's important to continuously monitor its performance and adjust as needed. Automation tools are meant to save you time and resources, so if they're not doing that, it might be time to reevaluate.

Don't Over-Automate: While automation can be a great asset, it's important not to overdo it. Some tasks, especially those that involve high levels of customer interaction, may be better handled by humans.

When implemented properly, automation can be a game-changer for your business, helping you work smarter, not harder. However, it requires careful planning, selection of the right tools, and continuous monitoring to ensure its success. As with all aspects of your business, the goal of automation should be to add value and enhance your operations, not complicate them.

Time to Oink!
Organize, Internalize, and Nurture the Knowledge!
Activity #1 – Let's Bake a Pie

Imagine, if you will, a bustling kitchen. The air is ripe with the sweet scent of apples and cinnamon, the clatter of utensils creating a symphony of productivity. This, my friends, is our company, and each month, we gather here to perfect our recipe for success, one process at a time.

Brainstorming: Each month, we should initiate a collective brainstorming session about a specific process. Here, every employee, contributes with new ideas. This stage is about free-thinking, creativity, and open dialogue - the first steps towards transforming our business processes.

Picture every employee as an ingredient in our apple pie of success. Each brings a unique flavor, a distinct texture, and an essential role to play. Our first step is to gather around the kitchen table, brainstorming ideas on how we can enhance the taste and texture of our pie - our business process. Every idea is a potential secret ingredient, waiting to transform our recipe.

Refinement: Next, we engage in a meticulous refinement process. We sift through the array of ideas, combining and narrowing them down to only the most promising ones.

Once we've gathered our ingredients, it's time to mix them together. We combine our ideas, blending them into a robust batter of innovation. We then sift through this mixture, narrowing down to the most promising flavors that will enhance our apple pie.

Challenging: At this stage, one employee assumes the role of the 'Doubter'. Their task? To question and challenge each idea, ensuring it can withstand scrutiny. This is our safeguard, our quality control, ensuring that every idea is robust and effective. Assign the Doubter role to a different person each month so that no one person gets stuck in a negative role.

Here, one of us steps up as the 'Taste Tester'. Their role is to challenge every flavor, every ingredient. They ensure our recipe can withstand the heat of the oven, and only the best ideas make it to the baking stage.

Documentation: Following this, another employee transcribes the proposed new or improved process. Their words serve as the blueprint for change, detailing the path towards enhanced efficiency and effectiveness. We assign this job to a single employee, and they become responsible for the follow-through.

The 'Chef' is named, tasked with writing out the new or improved recipe. They detail every step, ensuring the process is clear, concise, and ready for execution.

Implementation: Finally, we implement our new process. We test, review, and refine it, ensuring it not only meets but exceeds our expectations. Once perfected, it's launched into our daily operations.

We put our apple pie in the oven - we implement our new process. We watch it carefully, adjusting the temperature as needed, testing its readiness with a toothpick of scrutiny. We review, we refine, and when it's golden brown and delicious, we serve it - we launch our improved process.

Repetition: This cycle of analysis, refinement, and implementation isn't a one-off event. Regular reviews allow us to continually optimize all business processes, ensuring we stay dynamic, innovative, and ahead of the curve.

Remember, an apple pie is just one recipe in our cookbook of success. Regularly repeating this exercise ensures every recipe - every process - in our company is continually refined and improved.

This monthly endeavor isn't just about improving processes; it's about coming together as a team, creating a culture of innovation, and baking the best apple pie - the best company - we possibly can. As each process improves, our apple pie becomes more delicious, our company more successful. So, roll up your sleeves and get the whole team into the kitchen every month.

Activity #2 – Proven Time Management Methods

As a small-business owner, it's easy to get bogged down by the day-to-day tasks that keep your company afloat. With a limited amount of time, it's crucial for entrepreneurs to work smarter, not harder. Luckily, there are a handful of time management techniques that are tried and true and can help you save precious minutes and hours in your workday. Learn about these 10 techniques that can help you streamline your workload, increase productivity, and get more done in less time. Once you understand them, embrace one or two of these methods and make them your own.

Pickle Jar Theory: In 2002, the brilliant mind of Jeremy Wright introduced the groundbreaking Pickle Jar Theory. Also known as the Bucket of Rocks Theory or the Jar of Life Theory, this innovative technique revolutionizes how we prioritize tasks and responsibilities.

Imagine your typical day as a jar, and within it lies the key to unlocking maximum productivity and happiness. The jar represents the finite space of time, while the sand, pebbles, rocks, and even water, symbolize the various elements of our daily activities.

But how do we fill this jar effectively? The Pickle Jar Theory provides the answer. By understanding the order and time estimation needed for each task, we can optimize our daily routines.

Sand: these are the small, insignificant tasks that often distract and hinder our productivity. Social networking, mind-wandering, and unnecessary chatting with colleagues all fall under this category.

Pebbles: these tasks hold more significance than sand, yet they can be postponed or delegated. Phone calls, email responses, and meetings may seem urgent, but they can wait and should not overshadow the most crucial tasks.

Rocks: the absolute priorities. These tasks have long-term goals and severe consequences if left incomplete. Content writers focus on researching and writing, software developers tackle programming and testing, and every professional has their own set of essential tasks.

Water: the element of balance. This symbolizes our private life, the time spent with family and friends that is equally important in achieving overall happiness.

By adopting the Pickle Jar Theory, you can conquer your days with precision, achieve your goals, and find fulfillment in both your personal and professional life. Say goodbye to wasted time and hello to a harmonious existence.

Time Blocking Method: This method is all about scheduling your day into chunks of time, dedicating time to specific tasks. The idea is to assign blocks of time to certain activities, like checking and answering emails, client meetings, and project work. By doing this, you're able to stay focused on the task at hand and avoid distractions that can take up valuable time. Time blocking is a great way to ensure that you're dedicating enough time to each task throughout the day.

PPM Method: The PPM (Priority Pyramid Method) is a way of prioritizing tasks. Instead of seeing all tasks as equally important, the PPM assigns a value to them based on their priority. The idea is to focus on the tasks that will have the most impact on your business and move those to the top of the pyramid. The tasks that are less important can be left for later in the day or week. This method helps avoid getting bogged down by tasks that aren't as important and can help keep you focused on achieving your goals.

Pomodoro Technique: The Pomodoro Technique is a time management method that uses a timer to break your workday into 25-minute intervals, with a five-minute break in between. This technique is founded on the idea that working in bursts with short breaks can help boost productivity and prevent burnout. After four intervals, there's a longer break. This technique helps keep you focused and energized throughout the day.

Parkinson's Law: Parkinson's Law states that work expands to fill the time allowed for its completion. This means that if you give yourself an entire day to complete a task, it will likely take you the entire day to do it. If you give yourself a much shorter deadline, you'll be able to complete the same task in less time. The key to this method is setting realistic deadlines, so you're not setting yourself up for failure, but rather creating a sense of urgency to get things done.

Pareto Analysis: The Pareto Principle states that 80% of effects come from 20% of causes. In terms of business management, this means that 80% of your revenue can come from 20% of your clients. This principle can be used to evaluate how you're spending your time and prioritize tasks that are most valuable to your business. It can also help identify areas where you're spending too much time on tasks that aren't as profitable.

GTD Method: GTD (Getting Things Done) is a time management method that emphasizes capturing all your to-dos in a trusted system. The idea is to get everything out of your head and into your system, freeing up your mental energy to focus on the task at hand. With this method, you're able to capture everything that needs to get done, prioritize it, and organize it in a way that makes sense for you.

Eat That Frog Method: The Eat That Frog method is based on the premise that if you start your day by doing the most unpleasant or difficult task, the rest of your day will feel like a breeze. This technique helps overcome procrastination by tackling the task you're dreading the most first thing in the morning. By doing so, you're able to eliminate the stress and anxiety that can come from putting it off and boost your sense of accomplishment for the rest of the day.

Eisenhower Matrix: This simple but effective tool helps you prioritize tasks based on their importance and urgency. Dividing your tasks into four categories, urgent-important, non-urgent-important, urgent-non-important, and non-urgent-non-important, can help you clarify what needs your immediate attention and what can wait. This method helps you avoid doing urgent but unimportant tasks, which can often distract you from more important tasks.

SMART Goals: Creating SMART (Specific, Measurable, Achievable, Relevant, and Time-bound) goals will help keep you focused on what matters most, providing a roadmap for your business's success. Breaking goals into smaller and more manageable steps helps you stay on track and motivates you to reach each objective one by one.

Time management is essential for small-business success. By using these eight methods, small-business owners can take control of their time, increase productivity, and achieve their goals. Whether it's prioritizing tasks, scheduling your day with time blocks, or using the Pomodoro Technique to stay focused, there's a time management method that will work for everyone. By mastering these techniques, small-business owners can take their success to the next level and get more done in less time.

Download the Worksheets

Worksheet: Urgently Important
Worksheet: Active Listening
Worksheet: SMART Goals
Worksheet: Values and Vision

BLT

Begin Immediately, Learn Continuously, and Teach Others!

You've got a pile of materials. To the untrained eye, it might seem like a random collection of odds and ends. But you? You see potential. You see a rolling bar waiting to be built, a place of gathering, of camaraderie, of shared dreams and shared victories.

That pile of wood, nails, and screws? It's our business processes - diverse, varied, and brimming with untapped potential. To transform these scraps into a thriving bar, we need to analyze, understand, and optimize them. We need to become builders, architects of success, sculptors of efficiency.

Remember the acronym TEAM - Together Everyone Achieves More. It's not just a clever phrase; it's our guiding principle. Our team, like a skilled crew of builders, combines individual strengths to create something truly remarkable.

So, what happens when a team focuses on success? Magic. We convert raw materials into a masterpiece, dreams into reality. It's not about avoiding obstacles; it's about building over them. It's about moving forward, always forward, towards our shared vision.

Let's get motivated, let's get building. Let's gather around our processes every month, let's dissect and analyze them, let's uncover hidden efficiencies and untapped potential. Because a team that works together, wins together.

Are you ready to build? Ready to construct our path to success? Remember, today's processes are not a final project, they are just the beginning. So, let's put on our hard hats, grab our tools, and start building. Because together, we don't just chase dreams - we construct them.

Crew and Coaches

Your Employees, Contractors, Coaches, and Mentors:
They are the superstars of your small business, like the members of a rock band. Each one brings a unique skill set to the table, contributing to the overall harmony and success of the business. Without them, there's no music, just silence.

"If you want to build a ship, don't drum up people together to collect wood and don't assign them tasks and work, but rather teach them to long for the endless immensity of the sea."

— Antoine de Saint-Exupery

Chewing the Fat

Digging out of a Hole

I recall a joke about an old man traveling through a small town in the Midwest. This man was sitting outside a small café sipping his coffee. On the other side of Main Street, he saw two men working very hard. One man was digging holes every 10 feet or so, and the second man followed behind him refilling the holes with the displaced dirt. This went on for quite a while until curiosity got the best of the old man and he went over to ask them what they were doing. The first man said that this was all part of the Mayor's Beautification Program. He was part of a three-man team. He dug the holes, Barney planted the trees, and Earl filled the holes with dirt. The old man said, "But there's nobody planting trees! It's just the two of you!" The first man replied, "Just because Barney called in sick, doesn't mean that me and Earl can't do our jobs."

Now, take a moment to stop laughing and think about how this kind of misunderstanding happens far too often in some companies.

We've all encountered well-meaning employees who don't fully grasp the purpose of their role. We've seen managers who fail to understand the unique skills of their team members. There are countless business owners who haven't clearly communicated their beliefs, values, mission, and vision. And what's the point of having talented individuals and ambitious goals if there's no proper training or understanding of their purpose?

Your crew - your employees, contractors, coaches, consultants, and mentors - plays a crucial role in bringing your dreams to life. It's vital to have skilled individuals who align with your vision. But even more important is effectively communicating those dreams to your crew, so they feel informed, empowered, and truly appreciated.

Don't let misunderstandings hold you back. Build a strong crew, share your dreams with them, and watch as they help you soar to new heights.

The Appetizers

Building a Winning Crew: How to Create a Team that Aligns with Your Core Values

Every successful person knows that behind their triumphs and achievements is a great team of people who have supported them throughout their journey. Whether you're an entrepreneur, a leader, or a professional, you need a team to succeed. Building a winning crew is more than just hiring talented individuals, it's about creating a team that shares your vision, values, and passions.

When it comes to assembling a winning crew, the first thing you should do is to network and find Mentors and Coaches who can guide you along the way. Your mentors should be individuals who have business experience and are honest enough to provide critical feedback that can help you grow. A coach, on the other hand, should be someone who can help you develop your skills and expertise. They can teach you the tricks, shortcuts, and give you a fresh perspective on how to approach challenges. Mentors and Coaches don't necessarily have to be in the same industry as you, they must be able to understand your challenges and help you find ways to succeed.

Once you have your mentors and coaches, it's time to start building your core team. Hire people who not only have the experience and expertise you need but also have a passion for your goals. Look for individuals who share your values, work ethic, and can contribute to the culture you want to create. They should be team players who are willing to go the extra mile to ensure the success of the project.

Sub-contracting and farming out work are also a critical part of building a winning crew. Sometimes, you may need to outsource work that is outside your core competency to people and companies that have a proven track record on that specific task. When selecting who you work with, ensure that you do your due diligence to find reputable individuals or companies that can deliver quality work within your desired timeline. These people should be in line with your core values as well. This ensures that your goals are easier to understand and fulfilling them has a deeper meaning to all.

Training is also crucial to building a winning crew. Your team needs to be knowledgeable, skilled, and up to date with industry trends and innovations. Offering regular training and development opportunities can help sharpen their skills, expand their knowledge, and improve their performance. Make sure that you set clear expectations, provide the resources, and support they need, and offer feedback to help them grow.

Building a successful team takes time, effort, and resources. Remember, your crew reflects your mission, values, and vision. Choose wisely and hire individuals who have a passion for your goals and share your core values. Leverage the power of networking and find mentors or coaches who can help you along the way. Outsource work to reputable individuals or companies who can deliver quality work within your timeline. Train your team, offer feedback, and support their growth. Creating a winning crew takes effort but yields immeasurable benefits in the long run. With the right team by your side, you can conquer any challenge and achieve your dreams.

Building a strong team is the cornerstone of any successful business.

1. **Efficiency**: When a team works together, they can accomplish tasks faster and more effectively than individuals working on their own. Each team member brings unique skills and strengths

to the table, which can be leveraged to improve efficiency and productivity.

2. **Creativity and Innovation**: A diverse team can generate a wide range of ideas, leading to creative solutions and innovations. This can give your business a competitive edge in the marketplace.

3. **Motivation and Morale**: Working as part of a team can boost employee morale and motivation. It fosters a sense of belonging and recognition, which can lead to increased job satisfaction and productivity.

4. **Problem-Solving**: Teams are better equipped to solve problems than individuals. They can pool their knowledge and resources to find solutions more quickly and effectively.

5. **Learning and Development**: Teamwork promotes a learning culture where employees can learn from each other, share knowledge, and develop new skills.

6. **Shared Responsibility**: In a team, responsibilities are shared, reducing the pressure that someone working alone may feel. This can help to prevent burnout and improve work-life balance.

However, building a strong team isn't just about putting a group of people together - it requires careful planning, management, and leadership. It involves hiring the right people, fostering a collaborative culture, setting clear goals, and providing the necessary resources and support.

On the flip side, poorly planned team activities that don't consider employee interests or needs can lead to disengagement and resentment. So, it's important to carefully plan team activities and exercises that foster collaboration, boost morale, and improve communication.

In conclusion, a strong team can be a powerful asset for your business, driving efficiency, creativity, motivation, and success.

The Buffet

The Three Things Employees Need to GET from You to go from Good to Great!

If you want to keep your employees happy, it's essential to understand what they need. It's not enough to pay them well or offer benefits; you must give them clear expectations, empathy, and the tools to succeed. In this blog post, we will discuss the three things' employees need to GET from you to go from good to great: goals, empathy, and tools.

G - Goals: Employees need clear and specific goals to know what they are expected to achieve. Goals should be well defined, measurable, and achievable, and created together with the employee. By working together to create goals, you can ensure they are aligned with the company's objectives and that employees feel invested in achieving them. Make sure to revisit these goals regularly to evaluate progress, recognize successes, and identify areas for improvement.

E - Empathy: Your employees are human beings with feelings and emotions. When they are motivated, they can achieve great things, but when they are down, they might underperform. Empathy is crucial to understanding their needs and helping them through difficult times. It means being aware of their personal lives, showing appreciation, and being willing to listen. To cultivate empathy, make sure to regularly check in with your employees, listen to their concerns, and act when needed.

T - Tools: To perform their jobs well, employees need the right tools and resources. These can be anything from pens, paper, and computer programs to clear processes and procedures. Make sure to conduct regular inventory of the tools and resources your employees need and provide them with the necessary updates or upgrades. Additionally, review your processes and procedures to identify areas that require improvement or clarification.

To GET great employees and to GET them to stay, they need to GET what they need from you: goals, empathy, and tools. By setting clear goals together, showing empathy, and providing the necessary tools, you can create a work environment that employees thrive in. Remember to regularly check in with your employees to ensure that they are on track and feel valued. By doing so, you can minimize turnover, improve morale and productivity, and create a culture of excellence. GET it?

Recruiting the Right Employees: Strategies and Techniques

Recruiting the right people is a critical component of business success. The right people bring not only skills and experience, but also fresh ideas, diversity, and a cultural fit that can take your business to new heights. Here are some strategies and techniques:

1. **Clearly Define the Role**: Before you start recruiting, have a clear understanding of what the role entails. This includes the skills required, job responsibilities, and how the role contributes to your business goals.

2. **Use Multiple Channels**: In today's digital age, there are multiple channels you can use to reach potential candidates - from job boards and social media to networking events and recruitment agencies. Using a mix of channels can help you reach a wider pool of talent.

3. **Focus on Cultural Fit**: Skills and experience are important, but so is cultural fit. Look for candidates who align with your company's values and culture. These individuals are more likely to thrive in your organization and contribute positively to the team dynamic.

4. **Offer Competitive Compensation**: To attract top talent, you need to offer competitive compensation. This doesn't just mean salary - consider other benefits like flexible working hours,

professional development opportunities, and health and wellness programs.

5. **Sell Your Company**: Remember, recruitment is a two-way street. Just as you're evaluating candidates, they're evaluating you. Make sure to sell your company's vision, culture, and benefits to attract the best talent.

6. **Involve Your Team**: Your current team members can provide valuable insights during the recruitment process. They can help assess cultural fit and may even be able to recommend potential candidates.

7. **Don't Rush the Process**: It can be tempting to rush the recruitment process, especially if you need to fill a role quickly. But hiring the wrong person can be costly in the long run. Take your time to thoroughly evaluate candidates and make the right decision.

Remember, the goal of recruitment isn't just to fill a vacant role - it's to find the right person who will contribute to your business's success. As Steve Jobs once said, "The secret of my success is that we have gone to exceptional lengths to hire the best people in the world."

Retaining Talent: Creating a Positive Work Environment

Once you've hired great talent, the next challenge is retaining them. A high turnover rate can be costly and disruptive, and it can also impact team morale and productivity. Here are some strategies for creating a positive work environment that encourages employees to stick around:

1. **Create a Positive Culture**: A positive workplace culture can make employees feel valued and engaged. This includes elements like open communication, trust, mutual respect, and a sense of camaraderie.

2. **Provide Opportunities for Growth and Development**: Employees are more likely to stay with a company if they see opportunities for career growth and personal development. This could include training programs, mentoring, job rotation, teams, or opportunities for promotion.

3. **Recognize and Reward Good Work**: Regularly recognizing and rewarding employees for their hard work can boost morale and motivation. This could be in the form of verbal praise, bonuses, awards, or even small gestures like a thank you note.

4. **Offer Competitive Compensation and Benefits**: Fair and competitive compensation, along with benefits like health insurance, retirement plans, and paid time off, can make employees feel valued and appreciated.

5. **Promote Work-Life Balance**: Encouraging employees to maintain a healthy work-life balance can lead to increased job satisfaction and lower stress levels. This could include flexible working hours, remote work options, or wellness programs.

6. **Encourage Employee Feedback**: Regularly asking for and acting on employee feedback can make employees feel heard and involved. It can also provide valuable insights for improving your workplace.

7. **Lead by Example**: Leaders play a crucial role in creating a positive work environment. By demonstrating the values and behaviors you want to see in your team, you can set the tone for the entire organization.

Retaining talent involves more than just a good salary - it's about creating a work environment where employees feel valued, respected, and engaged. As Richard Branson said, "Train people well enough so they can leave, treat them well enough so they don't want to."

Retaining Talent: The STORCK Method

In the realm of business, talent is a driving force behind innovation, growth, and success. Retaining this talent, however, can often be a challenge. Enter the STORCK method, a strategy that focuses on key elements that employees value most in a workplace.

1. **SECURITY**: Job security is a fundamental need for many employees. It's not just about financial stability, but also the peace of mind that comes from knowing one's job is secure. To provide this, ensure transparent communication about the company's status and future, and establish clear, fair employment contracts.

2. **TRUST**: Trust is the bedrock of all successful relationships, including those in the workplace. Employees want to know they're trusted and that their work is valued. Foster this by giving them autonomy in their roles, involving them in decision-making processes, and maintaining open, honest communication.

3. **OPPORTUNITIES**: Everyone aspires. Providing opportunities for growth and advancement shows employees that you see their potential and are invested in their personal and professional development. This could include offering training programs, setting clear career paths, or providing mentoring and coaching.

4. **RESPECT**: Respect in the workplace goes beyond basic courtesy. It means valuing each person's ideas, knowledge, and experience. An open-door policy, where employees feel heard and appreciated, and a culture of inclusivity and diversity can foster a strong sense of respect.

5. **FAIR COMPENSATION**: While money isn't everything, fair compensation is crucial. Employees want to feel that their compensation reflects their hard work and contributions. Regularly review your compensation packages to ensure they're competitive and commensurate with employees' roles and responsibilities.

6. **KINDNESS**: Last but certainly not least, kindness. A positive, kind work environment can significantly boost employee satisfaction and morale. This can be cultivated through simple acts of appreciation, fostering a supportive team culture, and promoting work-life balance.

By addressing these six areas, you'll not only be able to attract top talent but also retain them, creating a thriving, productive workplace where employees feel secure, trusted, and valued. Remember, a happy employee is a productive employee!

Employee Retention Road Map

What information and direction are you giving your employees?

Does your culture emphasize reward for a job well done or a punishment for mistakes?

Do you have employees that are driven by reward or consequences?

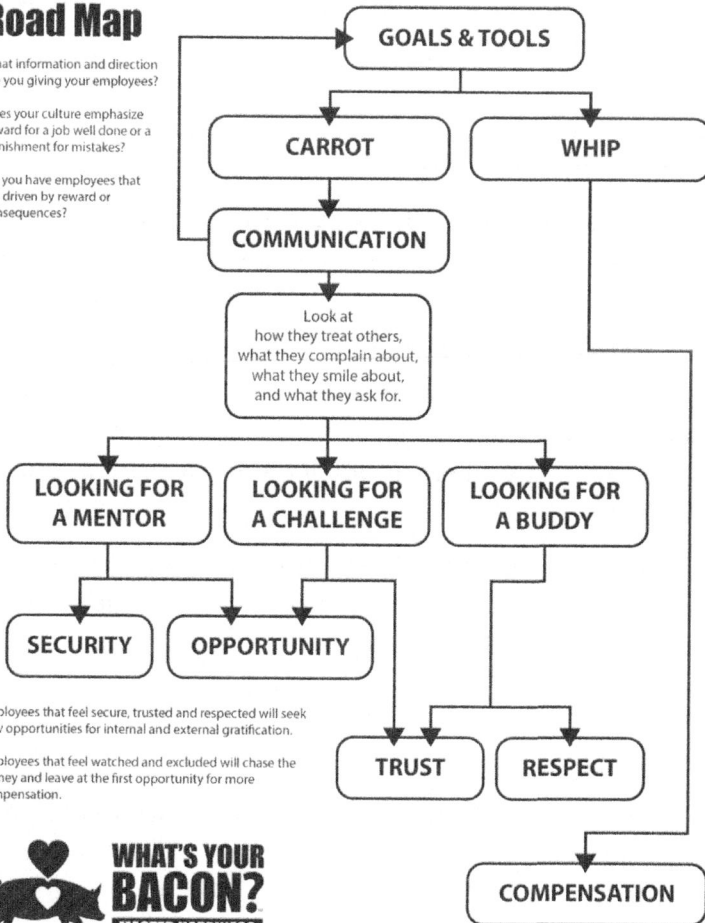

GOALS & TOOLS

CARROT

WHIP

COMMUNICATION

Look at how they treat others, what they complain about, what they smile about, and what they ask for.

LOOKING FOR A MENTOR

LOOKING FOR A CHALLENGE

LOOKING FOR A BUDDY

SECURITY

OPPORTUNITY

Employees that feel secure, trusted and respected will seek new opportunities for internal and external gratification.

Employees that feel watched and excluded will chase the money and leave at the first opportunity for more compensation.

TRUST

RESPECT

WHAT'S YOUR BACON?
MASTER HAPPINESS

COMPENSATION

When and How to Hire Freelance Contractors, Coaches, and Consultants for Your Business

In the dynamic world of business, sometimes you need a little extra help. That's where freelance contractors, coaches, and consultants come in. They can provide specialized skills, fresh perspectives, and temporary support that can drive your business forward. But when should you hire them, and how do you go about it?

When to Hire:

1. **Project-Specific Needs**: If you have a specific project that requires specialized skills your team doesn't possess, a freelancer or consultant could be the perfect solution. They can bring their expertise to the table and help complete the project efficiently and effectively.

2. **Short-Term Requirements**: If you need additional manpower for a short period, hiring a full-time employee may not be feasible or cost-effective. In such cases, bringing in a freelance contractor can be a smart move.

3. **Objective Insight**: Sometimes, you're too close to your business to see it objectively. A coach or consultant can provide an outside perspective, helping you identify areas for improvement and growth.

4. **Training and Development**: If your team needs to learn new skills or improve existing ones, a coach can provide tailored training and development programs.

How to Hire:

1. **Define Your Needs**: Before you start looking for freelancers or consultants, clearly define what you need. What tasks will they perform? What skills should they have? What are your expectations?

2. **Search for Candidates**: There are many ways to find freelancers or consultants. You can use freelance job platforms, professional networking sites, or even word-of-mouth recommendations.

3. **Evaluate Candidates**: Look at candidates' portfolios, read reviews from previous clients, and conduct interviews. This will help you assess their skills, work style, and whether they would be a good fit for your business.

4. **Discuss Terms**: Once you've found a potential candidate, discuss the terms of the contract. This includes payment, deadlines, communication methods, confidentiality, and any other expectations.

5. **Monitor Progress**: After hiring, keep track of the freelancer's or consultant's work. Provide feedback, address issues promptly, and maintain open communication.

Remember, each business is unique, so what works for one might not work for another. Consider your specific needs and circumstances before deciding to hire a freelance contractor, coach, or consultant.

Quick note about Vendors, Bankers, and Investors

In the journey of business growth, you're not alone. Your vendors, banker, and investors are key partners who can contribute significantly to your success. Building strong relationships with them is crucial for several reasons:

1. **Vendors**: These are your trusted suppliers of goods or services. A strong relationship with your vendors can lead to better pricing, favorable terms, and even exclusive deals. They can also offer valuable industry insights and advice. Moreover, reliable vendors ensure consistent quality and timely delivery, which directly impacts your customer satisfaction.

2. **Banker**: Establishing a good relationship with your banker can open a world of opportunities for your business. They can provide valuable financial advice, help you manage cash flow, and offer tailored financial products to support your business growth. In times of financial need, having a strong relationship with your banker can make obtaining loans or credit easier.

3. **Investors**: Investors are not just sources of capital. They can also bring in their expertise, network, and credibility. A strong relationship with your investors means they trust in your vision and are likely to support you in tough times. Regular transparent communication helps build investor confidence and can lead to further funding down the line.

So, how do you build these relationships?

1. **Communication is Key**: Regularly update your stakeholders about important developments, challenges, and successes. Be honest and transparent.

2. **Show Appreciation**: Simple gestures like saying thank you or acknowledging their contribution can go a long way in building strong relationships.

3. **Be Reliable**: Honor your commitments. Be it payment terms with vendors, loan repayments to your bank, or return on investment to your investors, reliability builds trust.

4. **Seek Advice**: Show them that you value their expertise. Ask for advice and consider their suggestions seriously.

5. **Meet Regularly**: Schedule regular meetings or catch-ups. This not only keeps everyone updated but also helps build personal connections.

Remember, business isn't just about transactions. It's also about relationships. The stronger your relationships with your vendors, banker, and investors, the more likely your business is to succeed.

Emphasizing Employee Communication: Tools, Techniques, and Best Practices

Effective communication is the backbone of a successful organization. It fosters a positive work environment, boosts productivity, and contributes to employee satisfaction. Here are some tools, techniques, and best practices for emphasizing employee communication:

Tools:

1. **Collaboration Platforms**: Tools like Slack, Microsoft Teams, or Google Workspace can facilitate real-time communication and collaboration among employees.

2. **Project Management Software**: Platforms like Asana, Trello, or Basecamp can help streamline project communication and keep everyone on the same page.

3. **Video Conferencing Tools**: Tools like Zoom or Google Meet are great for conducting virtual meetings, especially for remote teams.

4. **Employee Feedback Tools**: Platforms like SurveyMonkey or Google Forms can be used to gather employee feedback, which is a crucial part of two-way communication.

Techniques:

1. **Open-Door Policy**: Encourage an open-door policy where employees feel comfortable sharing ideas, concerns, or suggestions with management.

2. **BACON Meetings**: Conduct regular team meetings to discuss updates, challenges, and successes. This can also be a platform for employees to share their thoughts and ideas.

3. **Active Listening**: Practice active listening during conversations. This shows respect for the speaker's thoughts and encourages open communication.

Best Practices:

1. **Transparency**: Be transparent in your communication. Sharing company news, both good and bad, fosters trust and respect among employees.

2. **Timely Communication**: Communicate important information in a timely manner. This prevents rumors and misinformation from spreading.

3. **Two-Way Communication**: Encourage two-way communication. Give your employees a voice and show that you value their input.

4. **Recognition and Appreciation**: Recognize and appreciate your employees' efforts. This not only boosts morale but also encourages open communication.

Remember, effective communication doesn't happen overnight. It requires continuous effort and commitment. But with the right tools, techniques, and best practices, you can create a work environment where every voice is heard and valued.

Team Building

Building a successful business isn't just about having a great product or service - it's also about having a great team. And one of the ways to build a great team is through regular team activities and events. These activities can serve multiple purposes - they can boost morale, improve communication, foster creativity, and much more.

However, it's important to note that not all team activities are created equal. Poorly planned activities that don't consider the interests, needs, and comfort levels of team members can have the opposite effect, leading to disengagement and resentment.

So, how can young entrepreneurs implement effective team activities? Here are some tips:

Understand Your Team: Before planning any activities, take the time to understand your team. What are their interests? What motivates them? What are their working styles? This information will help you plan activities that are engaging and beneficial for everyone.

Set Clear Objectives: Every team activity should have a clear objective. Whether it's improving communication, fostering creativity, or simply boosting morale, having a clear goal will give direction to the activity and make it more meaningful.

Variety is Key: Mix up the types of activities you do. This could range from problem-solving exercises, and brainstorming sessions to social outings and volunteer work. A variety of activities will cater to different preferences and keep things interesting.

Encourage Participation, Don't Force It: While team activities are important, participation should never be forced. Make sure team members know that their participation is encouraged, but not mandatory.

Feedback is Crucial: After each activity, ask for feedback. What did the team enjoy? What didn't they like? What did they learn? This feedback will help you plan future activities that are even more successful.

Lead by Example: As a leader, your attitude towards team activities will set the tone for the rest of the team. Show enthusiasm, participate fully, and demonstrate the behaviors you want to see in your team.

Team-building activities should be inclusive, engaging, and purposeful. They should enhance collaboration, boost morale, and foster a sense of community within the organization. Here are some key points to keep in mind when developing your next event:

Inclusivity: Team building activities should never make an employee feel left out or uncomfortable. Activities that cater to a wide variety of interests and abilities ensure everyone can participate and contribute.

Engagement: The best team-building activities are those that captivate the team's attention and spark their creativity. This encourages active participation and engagement, leading to stronger bonds and improved communication.

Purposefulness: Every activity should have a clear objective. Whether it's improving problem-solving skills, encouraging creative thinking, or just letting off steam, the purpose should align with the team's needs and the organization's goals.

Here is a short list of popular team-building activities. Each has their unique benefits and appeal to different types of teams. It's essential to choose the one that fits your team best.

Scavenger Hunts and Escape Rooms are great for promoting problem-solving skills and teamwork. They require participants to collaborate and communicate effectively to succeed. This is ideal when you want to bring small groups of 3-4 people together. There is too much separation for larger groups.

Karaoke or Outdoor Adventures can be a fun way to get people out of their comfort zone. While there may be a few good singers, kayakers, and hikers, the focus should be on fun and participation rather than performance.

Parties and banquets are excellent for celebrating achievements and showing appreciation. However, it's crucial to recognize everyone's contributions to avoid feelings of exclusion or underappreciation.

Improv Comedy Workshops sound like a fantastic way to encourage effective communication, trust, and active listening. The "Yes, and" theory of improv is a powerful tool for fostering a positive and collaborative work environment.

Team activities can be a powerful tool for building a strong, cohesive team. But remember, the goal of these activities is not just to have fun - it's to create a team that communicates effectively, collaborates seamlessly, and feels valued and motivated. So, plan your activities with care, always keeping in mind the needs and interests of your team.

Time to Oink!

Organize, Internalize, and Nurture the Knowledge!

Activity #1 – Bringing us Together

The importance of having a company-wide meeting that focuses on the discussion and affirmation of the company's values, mission, and vision statement cannot be understated. Such a meeting is designed to help each team member gain a comprehensive understanding of the company's ultimate purpose and destination.

In these meetings, it is crucial that employees go beyond simply committing the company's values, mission, and vision statement to memory. They should be able to articulate each one clearly, highlighting how they and their colleagues have embodied these guiding principles in their professional conduct.

A significant feature of these meetings involves inviting random team members to take their turn in the spotlight. They are encouraged to stand up and define a value, subsequently recognizing another team player who exemplifies that value. This process is repeated with as many members as possible, fostering a sense of inclusivity and shared responsibility.

Starting your monthly and quarterly meetings in this manner serves a dual purpose. Firstly, it helps to reinforce a collective awareness of the company's guiding principles. Secondly, it nurtures a strong sense of community within the team, enhancing unity and a shared commitment to the company's objectives.

These company-wide meetings are not just about reiterating the company's guiding principles. They are about creating an environment where every team member feels valued and understood, where everyone is aware of the company's direction, and where everyone is united in the journey towards achieving the company's goals.

Activity #2 – Ours, Mine, Yours!

Recognizing and acknowledging that we are all unique individuals with distinct ambitions and aspirations is an integral lesson for everyone. Often, in the pursuit of the next big sale or deal, it's easy to overlook that our team members harbor dreams of their own. While we might wish for our entire team to be singularly focused on our objectives, it's essential to remember that they too have personal desires.

A practical approach to this is to categorize goals and aspirations into three distinct sections: the Company's Goals, Our Goals, and Their Goals. Begin by outlining what the company aims to achieve and explore potential strategies to reach these objectives.

Subsequently, take the time to articulate your personal ambitions. These could range from retirement plans to travel adventures, or simply more quality time with your family. Opening up about your goals sets a precedent for an open dialogue, demonstrating that it's perfectly normal to exhibit a bit of vulnerability.

Following this, encourage your team members to share their personal aspirations. These could include purchasing a new home or vehicle, innovating a novel product or process, or perhaps mastering a foreign language.

The final step involves engaging in a sincere discussion about our collective goals. Discuss your intent to assist them in achieving their dreams and express your hope for their support in realizing yours. Converse about how mutual assistance in accomplishing individual dreams can contribute significantly to the company's success.

This activity serves as a unifying force that humanizes everyone involved. It fosters a sense of harmony and strengthens our bond through a mutual commitment to continuous support. It underscores the fact that while we each have personal ambitions, we are also part of a larger team with shared objectives. And in helping each other succeed, we not only fulfill our individual dreams but also contribute to the collective success of the company.

Activity #3 – Making it Clear

Setting aside dedicated time to conduct a one-on-one meeting with each employee is an invaluable exercise. While this is particularly beneficial when onboarding new hires, it is equally essential to arrange these sessions with existing team members at the earliest opportunity. The primary objective of these meetings is to dispel any ambiguities and ensure that every employee fully comprehends the spectrum of their defined roles. This includes a clear understanding of what success entails, along with the compensation and rewards associated with outstanding performance.

During these meetings, take the opportunity to elaborate on their responsibilities. Discuss what the potential outcomes might be if they falter or excel in their roles. Emphasize how their actions can significantly impact others within the team and the company.

An effective method to confirm their comprehension of their role is to have the employee write down their job description in their own words. This not only assures you of their understanding but also gives them a clear picture of what is expected from them.

Impress upon them the importance of being a PRO - mastering their P - Priorities, understanding their R - Responsibilities, and recognizing O - Opportunities for self-improvement. This will not only enhance their personal growth but also contribute to the company's success.

Communicate to them that you are offering two promises, in exchange for one promise from them. Recognizing that it's unlikely they will remain with the team indefinitely, as new opportunities arise, personal needs and desires shift, and sometimes the evolution of industries and employees separates.

However, while they are part of your team, you pledge to cultivate an environment where they can feel fulfilled and experience growth. Should the day come when they decide to move on, you aim to make their decision difficult due to the fulfilling experiences and support you have provided. Your second promise is that, even after they depart, they will reflect on their time spent with us as a rewarding learning journey.

In return, all you ask is for their utmost effort and dedication in their roles, so much so that you would wish for them to remain with the team indefinitely.

Activity #4 – The BACON Meeting

Most employees would rather pour their hearts out to complete strangers than confide in their own managers. A scary thought, isn't it? The people who are in the best position to fix problems - the management - are often the last ones to hear about them. Instead, your employees are sharing their grievances with their peers and customers, inadvertently casting a shadow over your business. It's not an everyday occurrence, but it's happening more frequently than you'd like.

The answer lies in communication - the golden key that unlocks potential and solves problems. But without a well-designed and consistent communication strategy, your conversations will slowly become boring, unproductive, and useless. That is why you should have regular BACON Meetings with your employees.

B - The Big Picture: Start by focusing on your employees. How are they feeling? Motivated, demotivated, or indifferent? What's stirring in their minds and hearts? This is your opportunity to gauge everyone's emotional temperature. You're not discussing others, just the person in front of you. This shows empathy, care, and respect.

A - Action Steps and Goals: Still centered on the employee, what are their personal goals and the actions they plan to take to reach them? If they're riding high, how can they harness their positivity to become even better? If they're feeling low, what's their game plan to turn things around? This also serves as the perfect time to review their action steps and goals from the previous BACON Meeting. Do they need your support?

C - Conflicts, Concerns, and Solutions: Now, shift the focus to 'US'. What's happening within the business? Are we collaborating effectively? Could processes be improved? Are the company's goals crystal clear? This isn't a gripe session; it's an opportunity to identify potential issues and propose solutions. Remember to follow up on their ideas, creating a culture of mutual respect, trust, and a thriving work environment.

O - Other Stuff: Time to discuss external factors that could impact the company's growth. Are there any upcoming vacations or days off? What's the buzz in the industry or amongst our competitors? Your employees are your eyes and ears, brimming with valuable insights that can guide your decision-making process.

N - Notable Wins: Conclude the meeting on a high note, celebrating your employee's achievements. What have they done that deserves a round of applause? Maybe they exceeded a sales target or learned a new skill. Encourage them to share their victories, no matter how modest they might be. Their wins are wins for the entire team.

The BACON Meeting Worksheet isn't just a template; it's a pathway to understanding your employees, strengthening team dynamics, and steering your company towards a brighter future. Implement it, and you'll create a company culture that sizzles with positivity and productivity!

Activity #5 – Your Inner AHAB

Have you ever found yourself so engrossed in a task or project that everything else seemed to fade into the background? You were completely absorbed in the task at hand, moving forward with perfect rhythm and laser-like focus. Time seemed to lose all meaning, and you were simply in the ZONE. This state of deep immersion and intense concentration is what Mihaly Csikszentmihalyi, an eminent psychologist, refers to as FLOW. It represents a state of heightened focus and total engagement in an activity, whether it be art, work, or play. FLOW is intrinsically linked to a sense of euphoria or ecstasy, a state where true happiness can flourish.

The fundamental concept behind FLOW is the belief that individuals perform at their best when they are challenged to work on projects that align with their interests and skills. Conversely, when challenges, desire, and skills are low, individuals may become disinterested and apathetic. The objective of the Team Leader should be to encourage your team members to enter this ZONE periodically, facilitating significant strides in progress. However, it's crucial to strike a balance; setting challenges that are too strenuous, continuous, or unattainable can lead to burnout.

For Sales Teams, the Inner Ahab worksheet is an invaluable tool designed to help you identify potential sales opportunities. This worksheet, available for download at the end of this chapter, provides a structured approach to analyze and prioritize sales prospects.

Begin by listing ten customers in Quadrant (1). These are your loyal customers who provide recurring revenue. They are the backbone of your business - your Bread and Butter. Make sure to safeguard these relationships. Next, identify five potential sales opportunities and list them in Quadrants (2) and (3). These Could Bees and Should Bees represent your company's growth opportunities. If you're aiming for business expansion, it's worthwhile to invest a considerable amount of your time and energy pursuing these two groups. Lastly, reserve Quadrant 4 for THE WHALE! This is your Dream Customer, the one you aspire to win over. Pursuing this customer will require you to elevate your offering and make a bold move. Quadrant 4 is where the real excitement lies!

It's time to set your sights on YOUR WHALE! Incorporate this worksheet into your regular sales meetings. Encourage your team to nurture the Bread and Butter, relentlessly chase the Could Bees and Should Bees, and aim for the Whale. Every salesperson should have a Whale, a destiny, an improbable fish to pursue. This shouldn't just be an easy prospect; it should present a genuine challenge. Foster a collaborative environment where team members can share ideas and strategies to help each other land the big fish (even though we know a whale isn't technically a fish).

In due course, you'll discover that by targeting Whales, you inevitably reel in a considerable number of smaller fish. And that, after all, is the essence of sales success.

Activity #6 – Finding the Holes

So, you've assembled what you believe is a top-tier team, but things aren't quite falling into place as you'd hoped. Having a group of highly skilled individuals doesn't necessarily translate into a successful team. You may have a collection of talented individuals, but are they the right mix to form a cohesive, effective unit? Who might be missing from your lineup? Do you have all the roles filled with the right players?

To navigate this conundrum, let's identify the five integral roles that need to be filled in any successful team:

B - The Budget Baron. This role is akin to the custodian of the company's finances. The Budget Baron is vigilant, ensuring that revenue exceeds expenses. They are our bookkeepers, bankers, and accountants who keep a keen eye on the financial pulse of the organization.

A - The Architects and Artists. These are the creative minds and hands that conceive and construct the products and services your company sells. They are the engineers, production teams, manufacturers, and purchasing agents who bring your offerings to life.

C - Customer Cheerleaders. These individuals champion the cause of your customers. They engage with those who buy your products and services, uncovering their needs and desires. This valuable information fuels the company's growth. These roles are often filled by marketing, sales staff, and customer support personnel.

O - Optimistic Dreamers. These forward-thinkers are always looking towards the horizon, asking what could be possible. They are the visionaries of the company's future, often found in R&D departments or serving as the Company Coach.

N - The Navigator. This individual is at the helm, making crucial decisions. The buck stops with them. They are your team leaders, managers, and CEO.

Now, take a moment to reflect. Do you have these roles filled within your teams? Are you trying to wear too many hats? Is it feasible for you to handle all these tasks single-handedly? Have you placed the right people in the right positions?

Let's delve deeper into your team's composition and identify potential gaps. Drawing inspiration from "The Motivational Code" by Todd Henry, we can understand that individuals are motivated in six distinct ways. Each person will exhibit varying degrees of each motivation type, and it's important to view these not as weaknesses but as unique superpowers. Understanding where people fit, what motivates them, and how they thrive is fundamental to building a robust team.

B - Believers are visionaries, captivated by future possibilities while often overlooking the present. They play a vital role in guiding the company's evolution.

A - Achievers flourish under pressure, even though they may not be the best planners. You can rely on these individuals to get the job done.

C - Collaborators are the epitome of team players. They take collective failures personally and don't crave the spotlight.

O - Optimizers are more interested in finding better ways to do things than simply getting the job done. These individuals excel at refining processes and streamlining workflows.

N - Narcissists love the limelight and will happily claim all the credit for a team's success. Sometimes, you need that extra dash of audacity to clinch a deal and achieve your goals.

S - Scholars prefer to gather all possible information before making a decision. They serve as the company's safety net, ensuring any discrepancies are addressed internally before your products reach the customer.

Utilize the Motivational Code Worksheet to profile each employee. Try to determine which motivational code they primarily align with. This exercise will quickly reveal any gaps in your team and areas where you may be overstaffed. Then, it's up to you to evaluate whether everyone is in the right role, if anyone needs to be transitioned out, and where new hires would best fit in. Remember, forcing individuals into roles that don't suit them is a recipe for disaster. Instead, aim to align roles with individual strengths and motivations for a harmonious, productive team.

Download the Worksheets

Worksheet: Setting Goals
Worksheet: Feel the Flow
Worksheet: Your Inner Ahab
Worksheet: Motivational Code
Worksheet: Retention Map
Worksheet: Our, Mine, Yours

BLT

Begin Immediately, Learn Continuously, and Teach Others!

Entrepreneurs, Dreamers, and Doers. I'm here to tell you a tale. A tale about the importance of communication, understanding, and shared purpose in our businesses. It's a tale that starts with YOU.

You see, there's a magic to be found in every small business. It's not in the products we sell or the services we provide. It's in our people - our employees, subcontractors, coaches, mentors, and even ourselves. Each one of us brings something unique and valuable to the table. We each have our own dreams, skills, and motivations. And when we come together, united by a shared purpose, that's when the magic happens. That's when we become more than just a business, we become a TEAM.

But how do we unlock this magic? How do we transform a group of individuals into a cohesive, effective team? The answer lies in communication and understanding. We must learn to understand the needs and skills of our team members, to appreciate their individual talents and ambitions. And we must create an open and ongoing dialogue about the purpose and goals of our company.

Imagine a symphony orchestra. Every musician plays a different instrument, but they all play the same music. They each have a part to play, and they understand how their part fits into the whole. The conductor doesn't just wave his baton and expect music to happen. He communicates with his musicians; he understands their skills and their needs. He guides them, encourages them, challenges them. And together, they create something beautiful.

So, let me ask you this: Are you ready to be the conductor of your own symphony? Are you ready to unlock the magic in your team?

Now is the time, my fellow entrepreneurs. Now is the time to start communicating, to start understanding. To start appreciating the unique talents and ambitions of your team members. To start having open and ongoing discussions about the purpose and goals of your company. To start recognizing the value and importance of each member of your team.

So, let's do it. Let's unlock the magic in your teams. Let's create your symphony. Let's BE more than just a business. Together, we can achieve greatness. Because remember, a business is just a building. It's the people inside who make it a success.

The world needs more dreamers, more doers, more achievers. The world needs YOU!

Obstacles & Objections

Preparing for Obstacles, Opposition, and Objections: *This is like having a map when going on a treasure hunt. It helps you anticipate challenges, plan your route, and stay focused on the prize. Without preparation, your small business journey could end up like a pirate's - lost at sea!*

"Obstacles are those frightful things you see when you take your eyes off your goal.

— Henry Ford

"Obstacles don't have to stop you. If you run into a wall, don't turn around and give up. Figure out how to climb it, go through it, or work around it.

— Michael Jordan

Chewing the Fat

Peeking and Peaks

Embarking on a mountain climbing adventure may seem daunting, especially for someone like me who has never tried it before. However, my old friend, who was once an avid climber, used to share his exhilarating stories about the challenges, the excitement, and the preparations involved. The common thread in all his tales was the thrill of the journey, finding joy in the attempt. While reaching the summit was the Ultimate Goal, it was crucial to navigate through Mother Nature's surprises and embrace the entire adventure.

Climbing a mountain is not a smooth walk in the park; it's filled with steep slopes, rugged rock formations, and sharp edges. But it's precisely these obstructions that provide us with something to hold onto as we chance climbing to the top.

Sometimes in life, we tend to blow things out of proportion, turning molehills into mountains. Regardless of their size, we must confront and overcome these obstacles. When faced with adversity, some might give up and turn back. Others might find a way around or dig through their mountains. But there are a few individuals who are determined enough to climb over them.

During our ascent, we will constantly encounter tests that push us to our limits. It's easy to surrender and let go. Fatigue often sets in, leaving us feeling hopeless and looking up at those who are already above us. This can easily lead to discouragement.

Instead, I want to encourage you to take a moment to look back and appreciate how far you've come. There are people below you who haven't even reached your level yet. Extend a helping hand, lift them up, and push them beyond your achievements. And who knows, they may just be there to support your success as well.

It's crucial to remember that life is not a solitary mountain; it's a range of mountains. Reaching the peak is not the end of our journey, it is only one of the many awe-inspiring accomplishments in our lives. When we reach the summit, we gain a clearer perspective of the challenges that lie ahead. We can apply the lessons we've learned from overcoming past obstacles to conquer future ones. Each mountain we conquer will make the next ascent easier, each problem we face will become more manageable, and each failure will become an opportunity for growth and learning.

The Appetizer

Overcoming Obstacles One at a Time

Obstacles are a part of life, but they can feel overwhelming when striving for success in your personal or business life. From intense competition to a lack of knowledge, obstacles can take many forms, both tangible and intangible. However, the key to overcoming them is to identify and address them head-on. Let's discuss the importance of recognizing obstacles, the different types of challenges you may face, and strategies for overcoming them.

Identifying Obstacles

The first step in moving past obstacles is identifying what they are. Without recognizing the barriers in our path, we can't take action to overcome them. These obstacles can take on many forms, including market demand, financial constraints, and stiff competition, to name a few. However, less tangible obstacles like fear, procrastination, and a lack of knowledge can be even more challenging to identify and address.

Types of Obstacles

Once you've identified your obstacles, it's important to categorize them. Understanding the types of obstacles, you're facing can help create a strategy for tackling them successfully. One way to categorize obstacles includes external and internal challenges. External obstacles, like market competition and technological advancements, are often out of our control. In contrast, internal obstacles include a lack of motivation or fear of success and can be addressed through personal growth and mindset shifts.

Strategies for Overcoming Obstacles

Once you've identified internal and external obstacles, it's time to develop a plan to address them. For external obstacles, consider researching and forecasting market trends, collaborating with other businesses, seeking advice from industry experts, and leaning on your coaches and mentors. Internal obstacles, on the other hand, may require shifts in mindset, delegation, or hiring supportive team members. No matter the obstacle, approaching it with a growth mindset can lead to positive outcomes and improved business or personal success.

The Importance of Persistence

When it comes to facing obstacles, persistence is key. Even with a solid plan in place, overcoming obstacles often involves trial and error. Delayed progress or setbacks can be discouraging, but perseverance helps to keep us moving forward. Remember that obstacles can often be turned into opportunities for growth and learning.

Obstacles can present significant challenges when pursuing success in any aspect of life. However, recognizing and addressing these hurdles can lead to personal and professional growth. By identifying your internal and external obstacles and developing a plan to address them, you are creating a pathway to success. Remember that obstacles are just mountains – as long as you keep moving forward and persist in your efforts to overcome them, you can eventually reach the top and enjoy the view.

The Buffet

Get PICKY - A Guide to Navigating Business Challenges

Running a business is a series of challenges. You're bound to encounter Problems, Issues, Conflicts, Kinks, and Yikes, so get PICKY about uncovering them and solving them. Understanding these challenges and how to address them can help you steer your business towards success.

1. **Problems**: Problems are inevitable in any business. They are specific situations or obstacles that pop up unexpectedly and disrupt normal operations. These could be anything from a technical glitch to a sudden shortage of materials. The key to dealing with problems is promptness and adaptability. Quick identification, analysis, and resolution of problems can minimize their impact on your business.

2. **Issues**: Unlike problems, issues are long-running challenges that persist over time. They could be operational inefficiencies, recurring customer complaints, or consistent underperformance by a team or individual. Addressing issues requires a systematic approach. This involves identifying the root cause, developing a plan of action, implementing changes, and monitoring progress.

3. **Conflicts**: Conflicts arise from disagreements among team members, departments, or even with customers or suppliers. They could be due to differing opinions, miscommunication, or competing interests. Effective conflict resolution strategies include open communication, active listening, empathy, and negotiation. Remember, not all conflict is bad. Handled correctly, it can lead to innovative solutions and stronger relationships.

4. **Kinks in Our Armor**: These are overlooked flaws or weaknesses that could potentially lead to failure. It could be a gap in skills, outdated technology, or a flawed business process. Regular

audits and reviews can help identify these kinks. Once identified, they should be addressed promptly to prevent them from turning into major issues.

5. **Yikes**: Yikes are emergencies or crises that require immediate attention. It could be a major product failure, a sudden loss of a key client, or a public relations disaster. Having a clear understanding of individual responsibilities, open communication, and a culture that focuses on teamwork will help you through these emergencies.

Remember, being PICKY isn't about focusing on the negatives. It's about being proactive, vigilant, and resilient in the face of challenges. After all, every challenge you overcome is a step towards growth and success.

It's crucial to be fastidious about uncovering and addressing problems and issues, no matter their size:

1. **Preventing Escalation**: Small issues can snowball into big problems if left unaddressed. By nipping problems in the bud, you can prevent them from escalating and causing more significant damage down the line.

2. **Maintaining Quality**: Consistently high quality is key to customer satisfaction. By being vigilant about identifying and solving problems, you can ensure your products or services maintain the standards your customers expect.

3. **Boosting Efficiency**: Even minor issues can hamper productivity and efficiency. By ironing out these kinks, you can streamline operations and make your business run more smoothly.

4. **Building a Learning Culture**: When you're proactive about identifying and resolving issues, you create a culture where mistakes are seen as learning opportunities. This fosters innovation and encourages your team to continuously improve.

5. **Enhancing Reputation**: Businesses that are diligent about solving problems are seen as reliable and customer centric. This can enhance your reputation and give you a competitive edge.

6. **Reducing Costs**: Unresolved issues can lead to inefficiencies, rework, and lost customers, all of which can cost your business money. By resolving issues promptly, you can reduce these unnecessary costs.

Being PICKY is not about finding fault – it's about finding solutions. It's about creating a business that's resilient, responsive, and always striving to be better. So, don't shy away from those problems, issues, conflicts, kinks, and yikes – embrace them as opportunities to learn, grow, and succeed.

Overcome Obstacles by Creating a Sense of Pride

"Choose a job you love, and you'll never have to work a day in your life" – Confucius.

But it takes more than love to stay committed and excel in your job. It requires a sense of PRIDE that drives employees to perform their best every day. As a small-business owner, you have the power to instill that sense of PRIDE in your employees by giving them challenges and accountability. Give them a purpose in their work, goals, and the opportunity to solve problems. Fulfilling work does not come from a list of tasks, it is found in feeling necessary, valued, trusted, and relied upon.

Be sure that your team knows what you need from them and how their contribution is necessary to our overall success.

1. **Priorities:** One way to promote pride among your employees is by setting priorities that align with your business goals. Priorities provide a clear roadmap for employees and keep them focused on what is essential. Take the time to explain the reasoning behind each priority and how it contributes to the company's overall vision. When employees understand the significance of their tasks, they are more likely to feel invested and prideful in their work.

2. **Responsibilities:** Employees should have a clear understanding of their roles and responsibilities. When they know what is expected of them, they can work efficiently and operate with autonomy. Ensure that you provide the necessary training and resources to help them excel in their positions. Acknowledge when they meet or exceed expectations and provide constructive feedback when needed. Establishing open communication and trust with your employees can contribute significantly to developing pride in their jobs.

3. **Interruptions:** Interruptions are inevitable, but they can have a significant impact on productivity and morale. Employees with a deep sense of pride can handle interruptions and challenges better. As an employer, you can help by creating an interruption-free environment or introducing systems that minimize disruptions. Encourage your employees to tackle interruptions with an attitude of problem-solving instead of frustration.

4. **Duties:** Small, less glamorous tasks are a part of any job, but they can still contribute to the success of your business. Acknowledge the importance of these smaller jobs and let your employees know that their contributions are valued. Encourage them to take pride in their attention to detail, processes, and routine tasks. Small wins can lead to a sense of accomplishment and pride in one's work.

5. **Endeavors:** Encourage your employees to take on tasks that interest them and can contribute to personal and professional growth. By allowing them to explore new areas, you can foster a culture of learning and innovation. It's also essential to

recognize and appreciate when employees go above and beyond the job scope and achieve exceptional results. Acknowledging their accomplishments helps foster a sense of pride and demonstrates that their hard work does not go unnoticed.

Creating a sense of pride in your employees goes beyond compensation and benefits. It requires effort, dedication, and a leader who is invested in their team's success. By promoting a sense of purpose and pride in every task, big or small, you can help your employees feel valued and engaged. This, in turn, can lead to better productivity, higher morale, and a positive company culture. As a small-business owner, you have the power to create an environment where employees take pride in their work and the success of your business.

Obstacles for Small Businesses: Insights and Solutions

Running a small business can be rewarding, but it's not without its challenges. Here are some common obstacles that small businesses often face, along with potential solutions:

1. **Finding Customers**: Attracting customers is one of the most significant challenges for small businesses. A strong marketing strategy, targeted advertising, and a robust online presence can help attract potential customers.

2. **Increasing Brand Awareness**: Building a brand that resonates with your target audience can be a challenge. Collaborating with influencers, leveraging social media, and creating valuable content can boost your brand's visibility.

3. **Lead Generation**: Generating quality leads is crucial for business growth. This could involve optimizing your website for SEO, using email marketing effectively, or investing in pay-per-click advertising.

4. **Lack of Funds**: Financial constraints can limit a small business's growth. Exploring different funding options like small business loans, crowdfunding, or finding investors can help overcome this challenge.

5. **Time Management**: Juggling multiple tasks can lead to burnout. Using time management tools, delegating tasks, and setting clear priorities can help manage time more effectively.

6. **Recruitment and Retention**: Finding and retaining the right talent can be difficult for small businesses. Offering competitive compensation, fostering a positive work culture, and providing opportunities for growth can attract and retain quality employees.

7. **Balancing Growth and Quality**: Rapid growth can sometimes compromise quality. Implementing effective quality control measures and scaling operations mindfully can ensure consistent quality even during growth.

8. **Cash Flow Issues**: Managing cash flow can be tricky for small businesses. Regular financial forecasting, timely invoicing, and managing expenses efficiently can help maintain a healthy cash flow.

9. **Supply Chain Issues**: Disruptions in the supply chain can impact business operations. Building strong relationships with reliable suppliers and maintaining a buffer stock can mitigate supply chain risks.

10. **Inflation and Price Increases**: Rising costs can squeeze profit margins. Regularly reviewing pricing strategies, improving operational efficiency, and diversifying suppliers can help manage cost increases.

Overcoming these obstacles requires strategic planning, resilience, and adaptability. With the right approach, these challenges can be turned into opportunities for growth and success.

Creating Systems for Solving Emergencies and Long-Term Problems in Business

Creating effective systems for solving both emergencies and long-term problems is crucial for any business. Here's a step-by-step guide to creating such systems, rooted in trust, inspiration, and open communication:

1. **Identify the Problem**: The first step in problem-solving is recognizing that there is a problem. This involves being vigilant and regularly reviewing business operations. Use tools like customer feedback, employee input, and performance data to identify areas of concern.

2. **Define the Problem**: Once a problem has been identified, it's important to understand it fully. What is causing the problem? Who and what is affected by it? Answering these questions can help you define the problem clearly and set the stage for finding solutions.

3. **Brainstorm Potential Solutions**: Encourage your team to discuss and brainstorm potential solutions. Foster an environment where every idea is welcomed and considered. The more diverse the ideas, the better the potential solution.

4. **Analyze and Select the Best Solution**: Not all solutions will be viable or effective. Analyze the pros and cons of each proposed solution. Consider factors like cost, time, resources, and impact on other areas of the business. Then, select the solution that best addresses the problem.

5. **Develop a Plan**: Once a solution has been chosen, create a detailed action plan. This should include specific steps, responsibilities, timelines, and resources needed. Ensure everyone involved understands the plan and their role in it.

6. **Execute the Plan**: Implement the action plan, ensuring everyone is clear on their tasks. Monitor progress closely and provide support where necessary. Remember, open communication is key during this stage.

7. **Review and Learn**: After implementation, review the results. Did the solution solve the problem effectively? What could have been done better? Use these insights to improve your problem-solving process for future issues.

Remember, every problem is an opportunity to learn and grow. By creating robust systems for problem-solving, you can turn challenges into steppingstones towards business success.

Facing Opposition with SWOT

Analyzing your strengths and weaknesses, as well as those of your competition, along with identifying opportunities and threats, is a crucial step in strategic business planning. This process is commonly known as a SWOT Analysis (Strengths, Weaknesses, Opportunities, Threats). Here's a step-by-step guide on how to conduct a SWOT analysis:

1. **Identify Your Strengths**: These are the things that your business does exceptionally well. It could be a unique product feature, a highly skilled team, strong brand recognition, or proprietary technology. Consider what sets you apart from your competitors.

2. **Recognize Your Weaknesses**: These are areas where your business could improve. It could be a lack of resources, outdated technology, a weak online presence, or poor customer service. Be honest and open about your weaknesses.

3. **Analyze Your Competition**: Research your main competitors. What are their strengths? Where do they outperform you? This will give you an idea of what you're up against. Similarly, identify their weaknesses. These are areas where you can gain a competitive edge.

4. **Identify Opportunities**: Look for untapped potential in your market. This could be a new trend, a change in regulations, a gap in the market, or a potential partnership.

5. **Spot Threats**: These are external factors that could harm your business. It could be a new competitor, changing consumer preferences, economic downturns, or negative publicity.

Once you've conducted your SWOT analysis, use it to develop a strategic plan. Leverage your strengths and opportunities to grow your business. At the same time, work on improving your weaknesses and prepare for potential threats.

Remember, a SWOT analysis is not a one-time activity. Regularly reviewing and updating your SWOT analysis can help you adapt to changes in your business environment and stay ahead of your competition.

Overcoming Objections in Sales - Why They Won't Buy

As a small business owner, you know that every sale is important. But have you ever stopped to consider the reasons behind a lost sale? Understanding objections from potential customers can provide valuable insights into where you can improve and help increase sales.

Before we dive into the five most common objections, it's important to start with a critical step: qualifying the customer. Take the time to learn about their needs and goals. If you try to sell to someone who doesn't need or want your product or service, you're wasting your time and theirs. Don't rush the sales process, build relationships with your customers, and turn objections into sales opportunities.

"No Need" is the most crucial objection. If a customer doesn't see the need for your offering, why would they buy it? To combat this objection, you need to present a clear value proposition that communicates how your product or service will solve their specific problem. You should pre-qualify your leads before trying to convert them into a sale. If you promote your product to the wrong audience, you'll be able to attract traffic and nurture a relationship, but you won't be able to make a sale.

"No Desire" is like "No Need." The customer may understand what your product does, but they're not sold on why they should care. You need to show them how your product can change their lives for the better and create a sense of obsession to motivate them to buy. Create compelling marketing campaigns by knowing your audience.

"No Trust" is simply a lack of confidence in your business or product. To overcome this objection, you need to earn their trust and build credibility. Ways to do this includes providing a satisfaction guarantee, testimonials to prove your claims, and to provide social proof. Scammer businesses are high; it makes many consumers wary of them. Show testimonials from happy customers and even influencers in the industry to prove that you're trustworthy.

"No Rush" can be due to several reasons, including financial constraints or indecisiveness. You must create a sense of urgency. Offering temporary discounts, deals or add-ons can be an effective way to motivate buyers to act quickly. Use images of scarcity to trigger an opinion that your product is one-of-a-kind. Ensure you have a strong positioning voice that informs potential customers that prices will increase, or availability will disappear over time.

Lastly, **"No Value"** means the customer feels the product is too expensive for its quality. Your job is to demonstrate the value of your product. Help them see the benefits of investing in your product or service instead of running with generic commodities and explain what the return of investment is. Money in the bank is what businesses want, and that's what customers are often looking for.

Objections can be frustrating for small business owners, but they can provide valuable insights into why customers may be hesitant to buy. The key is to listen to their objections and use them as an opportunity to demonstrate the value of your product or service. Understand each of the five objections and prepare for each of them before you jump into the sales cycle. Always remember, celebrate every win, and learn something from every NO so that you can come back sizzling, smarter and stronger than ever before.

Time to Oink!
Organize, Internalize, and Nurture the Knowledge!

Overcoming Obstacles as a Team

Business meetings are an integral part of any organization. They are essential for reviewing progress, addressing issues, setting goals, and making important decisions. But let's face it; not all meetings are productive. For many small-business owners, meetings often turn out to be a waste of time and resources, with little or no results. The good news is we can make our business meetings more purposeful and productive with a few essential tips.

Have a Defined Purpose

The first essential tip to improving your business meetings is to have a clear goal or purpose for each meeting. Before scheduling any meeting, ask yourself what the meeting's objective is and what you hope to accomplish at the end of it. By being clear on the meeting's purpose, you will be able to set a clear agenda, invite only the necessary people and ensure that the meeting doesn't deviate from its intended purpose.

Opportunities for All to Talk

The best meetings are those that provide an opportunity for all attendees to express their ideas and feedback. As a small-business owner, you should ensure that your meetings are not one-sided. Encourage everyone to speak up and contribute to the meeting's agenda. By giving everyone a chance to voice their opinions, you are more likely to get diverse and creative ideas.

Lean Toward More Interaction Than Lecture

Meetings that are more interactive are more productive than those where the presenter lectures throughout the session. To improve your business meetings, make sure you engage your attendees in the discussion rather than just presenting information. Encourage them to share their experiences and perspectives on the topic at hand.

Concentrate on Listening and Learning

One of the most overlooked aspects of meetings is listening. Meetings can be more fruitful if, as the host, you listen more than you talk. Listening involves paying attention to your participants, understanding their concerns, and addressing them during the meeting. Active listening helps to build trust among participants and demonstrates that you value their opinions.

Include a Next-Steps Strategy

The next-steps strategy is crucial for creating actionable items for every meeting. Your meeting should have a clear plan of what happens after the meeting. What steps will each team member take? Who is responsible for what? When is the next meeting? By creating a concise and straightforward plan for what happens after the meeting, you give your participants a sense of responsibility and ownership.

End with an Element of Fun or a Path towards Positivity

The last essential tip to improving your business meetings is adding an element of fun or positivity at the end of the meeting. It's essential to end your meetings on an encouraging note and leave your attendees feeling motivated. The little things can go a long way in creating positive energy in your meetings. It could be anything, from praising an individual's contribution, laughing at a lesson learned, or sharing an appropriate and amusing story.

Meetings are an essential part of any organization, but they don't have to be dull and unproductive. As a small-business owner, you can make your meetings purposeful and productive by following these essential tips. When you have a defined purpose, opportunities for all to talk and concentrate on listening and learning, you can have more engaging meetings. Planning a next-steps strategy and ending with confident optimism goes a long way in building a positive working culture in your organization. By implementing these essential tips, you can take your business meetings to the next level.

One on Ones - BACON Meetings

Having open communication between employees and management is crucial for the smooth operation of any business. One way to facilitate this is through regular BACON Meetings.

BACON Meetings, which stands for Big Picture, Action Steps and Goals, Concerns and Solutions, Other Stuff, and Notable Wins, are designed to cover a broad range of topics and create a two-way dialogue between employees and their supervisors.

Each employee should have a BACON Meeting with their supervisor twice per month, while supervisors should also have regular BACON Meetings with upper management.

Here's a breakdown of what each section of a BACON Meeting entails:

- **Big Picture**: This section focuses on the individual's personal experiences. It's an opportunity to discuss what's motivating or demotivating them and how they're feeling about work.

- **Action Steps and Goals**: Based on the Big Picture discussion, the meeting moves onto formulating action steps and goals. The aim is to leverage the positives and address the negatives.

- **Concerns and Solutions**: This part of the meeting focuses on issues related to other employees, customers, and policies. It's not a platform for complaints, but rather a chance to discuss problems and propose solutions to help the company evolve.

- **Other Stuff**: Here, the conversation shifts to external factors. What's happening in the industry that could affect the company? This helps keep everyone informed and prepared for potential changes or challenges.

- **Notable Wins**: The meeting concludes on a positive note by celebrating a recent success or achievement by the individual. This fosters a sense of accomplishment and boosts morale.

By implementing regular BACON Meetings, you can ensure open lines of communication, encourage active problem-solving, and foster a positive and inclusive company culture.

Team Meetings

Team meetings empower individuals to work with others to get more done. Teams are more than just departments, they are an overlap of employees tasked with sustaining, projecting, innovating, and evolving, and fulfilling the company's mission and vision. These meetings should happen at least once per month but can happen more often if needed.

Even though they work as a team, it is important to give individuals specific tasks that they are responsible for. A successful team is a group of individuals that pull and push the other members. There is no room for excuses or placing blame, we succeed, learn, and grow together.

Here is an agenda outline for your Monthly Team Meetings:

- **Progress Report** –This should be the first item on your agenda. All team members should come prepared to present their progress on various tasks and projects. This not only keeps everyone accountable but also provides a platform for sharing ideas and troubleshooting issues. Encourage each member to share what they have accomplished since the last meeting, what challenges they faced, and their plans for moving forward.

- **Pivot, Pause, Pursue** – The second item on the agenda should be to assess the current strategy and decide if any changes need to be made. You may find it necessary to pivot entirely, pause certain projects or initiatives, or pursue a new avenue altogether. This is a time for discussing what is working and what isn't and brainstorming new solutions if necessary. If we decide to pivot or pursue a different direction, who will take this as their responsibility? And if we agree to pause, decide a date that this issue will be revisited.

- **Provisional Partners** – Creating a strong team means being able to handle adversity. At each team meeting, pick one member, the "Nay Sayer," whose job is to politely challenge the ideas brought forth and identify any shortcomings in the plan. This person acts as a devil's advocate, and it's important that the rest of the team recognizes their value in this role. Additionally, each meeting should also include an "Outsider" – someone who is not typically part of the team. This person can bring a fresh perspective and help the team clarify their purpose.

- **Praise the Players** – As we near the end of the meeting let's take a moment for each member to call out another member on the team and recognize their contributions and successes. These meetings should be an opportunity to build camaraderie and team spirit, and recognizing individual efforts is essential for morale and motivation.

- **Plan Summary** – Before concluding the meeting, review the plan and highlight any specific action items that need to be completed before the next meeting. It may be helpful to revisit long-term goals and objectives to ensure that everyone is on the same page. End the meeting with a sense of excitement and momentum, reminding the team that they are working together towards a common goal.

Team meetings are a vital part of any successful small business. They provide the structure and framework necessary for collaboration, communication, and problem-solving. By following a monthly team meeting agenda, you can empower your team to work together effectively and efficiently, ensuring that everyone is working towards a common goal. Remember to recognize and praise individual efforts and be open to challenging each other for the sake of improvement. By creating a dynamic and supportive team, you can take your business to the next level.

Coaching Meeting

As a small-business owner, it can feel like you're juggling multiple tasks and responsibilities at once. From managing your team to ensuring customer satisfaction and handling finances, it's understandable how easy it is to forget about checking in with yourself and your company's progress. This is where regular coaching meetings come in. These meetings are an opportunity for you and your coaches to discuss your company's big picture, review goals, address concerns and solutions, and celebrate wins. In this blog post, we'll explain the benefits of regular coaching meetings and how they can help small-business owners stay on track. They follow the same structure as a BACON Meeting with more emphasis om ideation.

Here's a breakdown of what each Coaching Meeting includes:

- **Big Picture**: One of the main advantages of regular coaching meetings is the emphasis on the big picture. Taking time to discuss how you're feeling and how the company is progressing is an important aspect of self-reflection and can help you realign yourself and the company's goals. By checking in with your emotions and energy levels, you can determine whether you need to make changes or continue down the same path.

Additionally, discussing company progress provides insight into what is or isn't working and can help inform future decisions.

- **Action Steps and Goals**: Regular coaching meetings provide a dedicated space to review the Ultimate Goal, the 10-year goal, three-year goal, and the current year's goal. By reviewing these goals, you can determine whether you're on track or if a change in direction is necessary. Goal setting during coaching meetings helps to ensure that milestones are met while keeping everyone focused on the company's purpose and vision.

- **Concerns and Solutions**: By reviewing concerns brought forth by your team, you can work on creating actionable solutions. This means that issues can be resolved in a timely and efficient manner, improving team morale, and increasing productivity. Additionally, postponing and eliminating concerns that don't align with company goals and needs can help to streamline daily operations and reduce stress.

- **Other Stuff**: Forecasting the future is important in any business. Through regular coaching meetings, small-business owners can discuss future possibilities and create contingency plans for potential changes. By discussing "what if" and "if then" scenarios, small-business owners are better equipped to handle unexpected changes and setbacks. This also helps to reduce stress and promotes proactive planning.

- **Notable Wins**: Finally, celebrating successes is essential to maintaining motivation and momentum. Regular coaching meetings provide a space to review and discuss notable wins, lessons learned, big improvements, and surprise enhancements. By dedicating time to celebrate these successes, you're acknowledging that hard work pays off and that it's essential to move forward with a positive attitude.

Coaching meetings are an essential part of any small-business owner's routine. By taking time to reflect, review, address concerns, forecast the future, and celebrate success, small-business owners can maintain their focus and momentum. Regular coaching meetings provide a space for addressing concerns and solutions, forecasting the future, and reviewing notable wins. Ultimately, these meetings help small-business owners stay aligned with their company's purpose and vision while contributing to overall success and growth.

All Hands Meetings

At least once per year, get the entire company together. This is not the time to solve problems and issues. Instead take this opportunity to let your team know that YOU understand that these concerns exist and that WE are working to overcome them.

Here is a list of what needs to be accomplished in your annual All Hands Meetings:

- **Ice Breaker** – Not everyone from every department has an opportunity to meet the rest of the team. Mixing and matching people and getting them talking is a great way to bring the entire company together.
- **News** – New Employees, new titles, new processes, new launches. It's time to boast and brag about the growth and evolution of the company and the team members.
- **Activity** - Personal Growth Presentation or – Give them something to remember. Based on the size of the company, get your team to participate in an activity that will leave them thinking, feeling, and smiling. This could be a team-building activity, an inspirational presentation, or a workshop. Help them grow as individuals and they will grow as a team.
- **Q&A with Leadership Team** – Opening the floor to questions is an ideal way to demonstrate trust, transparency, and clarification.

- **Spotlight** – Recognize each Department and their successes in reaching goals, vision, and mission, or demonstrating company values.

Throughout all meetings you will see that the best practices are to go over progress first. Follow up with discussions of what the next steps should be and assign ownership when possible. Set completion dates and define what succeeding and failing means. Discuss what happens next and end with praise on performance.

Having these meeting regularly will ensure open communication and bring to light all Problems, Issues, Concerns, Kinks, and Yikes; how they will be handled and by who.

Download the Worksheets

Worksheet: Know Your Competition
Worksheet: Know Yourself
Worksheet: BACON Meetings
Worksheet: Defense
Worksheet: Objection Beater

BLT

Begin Immediately, Learn Continuously, and Teach Others!

Like a mountain climber gearing up for a challenging ascent, every small business owner embarks on an adventure that promises exhilarating highs and daunting lows. The path to success is seldom smooth or straightforward, but rather, it's a series of peaks and valleys, each one presenting its own unique set of obstacles and opportunities.

Mountains, much like the challenges we face in our businesses, can be intimidating. Their towering peaks seem insurmountable, their steep slopes treacherous. But remember, no mountain was ever conquered by merely staring at it from the base. It takes courage, determination, and a bold first step.

Every obstacle you face as a small business owner is a mountain waiting to be climbed. Each hurdle is a learning experience, an opportunity to grow, to adapt, and to become stronger. When you stumble, you learn. When you fall, you rise again, more resilient than before.

Just as mountaineers rely on their teams, know that you are not alone in your entrepreneurial journey. There is a community of fellow climbers—your team, your coach, and other small business owners—struggling, learning, and growing alongside you. Reach out, connect, and lean on each other for support.

Face your mountains. Embrace the climb. See each obstacle not as a roadblock, but as a steppingstone on your path to success. Strap on your gear, take a deep breath, and begin your ascent. Remember, the view from the top is worth every step of the journey.

You have the strength, the courage, and the determination to meet any challenge head-on. So, climb that mountain. Conquer your fears. Overcome your obstacles. The peak is within reach, and the world is waiting to see you at the top.

Narrative & Nudge

Your Narrative, The Way You Tell Your Story: *This is the blockbuster movie script of your small business. It captivates audiences, sets you apart from competitors, and connects you with customers on an emotional level. Without a compelling narrative, your small business is like a film without a plot - unlikely to be a box office hit.*

"I've learned that people will forget what you said, people will forget what you did, but people will never forget how you made them feel.

– Maya Angelou

"A brand is the set of expectations, memories, stories, and relationships that, taken together, account for a consumer's decision to choose one product or service over another."

— Seth Godin

Chewing the Fat:

Be the Goat

My Auntie Candy was a great storyteller. She got that nickname from bribing her many nieces and nephews with candy, and if she didn't have candy she would offer us a lint-covered antacid from the bottom of her purse. But I didn't need candy to look forward to her visits, I searched her out for her stories.

One of her favorite stories to share was a Norwegian fairytale called the "Three Billy Goats Gruff."

Long ago, three goats needed to cross a bridge to reach a grassy field, but a mean old troll lived underneath and threatened to eat them. The smallest goat crossed first, suggesting the troll wait for his bigger brother for a better meal. The troll agreed and the same happened with the middle-sized goat. The third goat came along, larger than the troll expected, they fought, and the troll ended up in the river. After that, the goats freely crossed the bridge to the meadow, showing that even a little goat with a good story can overcome tough obstacles.

When we tell stories, whether it's to entertain, persuade, or inform, we must know what we want our audience to take away. Here are the 5 key takeaways: Receive, Reflect, Remark, Remember, or Repeat.

Receive: Receiving a story simply means capturing the listener's attention, like the first goat distracting the troll. However, in business, we can't afford to waste our customer's time with pointless tales come and go.

Reflect: Reflection is about making our message resonate with the audience. Just like the second goat had to make the troll ponder, we want our clients to contemplate and feel something after hearing our stories.

Remark: Now remarking is taking it up a notch. It's when our message nudges the listener into action, just like the third goat challenging the troll. In business, we want our prospects to engage with us, ask questions, and show interest. Keep in mind, if our goal is not a win-win, someone is going to get all wet.

Remember: But here's the real magic: making your story unforgettable. To leave a mark, we need to create a brand, an identity, and an image that sticks in people's minds. Only then will they remember us and our message.

Repeat: And that brings us back to my incredible Auntie Candy, the true GOAT (Greatest of All Time). Her stories were so captivating that not only did people remember them, they couldn't help but share them with others. Just imagine creating a message or offer so compelling that your customers become your biggest advocates and repeat your tales over and over again.

It's time to craft the perfect story that will lead you and your customers to a happily ever after.

Sales is a piece of CAKE

My first and most impactful sales mentor was my mother. We were not a rich family, but my mother and father did everything they needed to do to make sure that we had food on the table and a roof over our head. My father worked construction and my mother did some bookkeeping, sold at the flea market, and was a great storyteller.

I remember us always having cake at the house. She said it was the right thing to do in case we ever had company. She used to tell me that great salespeople always served CAKE.

As a rebellious youth I turned my back on cake and became a "Pie-kind-of-Guy." I Told her that great salespeople always served PIE; it was warmer and more welcoming than the formality of cake. PIE: Persuading, Informing, and Entertaining.

She told me to think about people at a party. The Entertaining Person is always invited, and the crowd gathers around them quickly. The Informative Person attracts attention too because everyone wants to hear a little gossip from time to time. But if you are known as the Persuasive Guest, people will start avoiding you like turkey bacon (just a sorry imitation).

Great Salespeople serve CAKE.

C – Connect. The best salespeople are like skilled bakers, kneading dough with care and patience. They take the time to understand their customers, to find common ground, to build genuine relationships. They know that trust is the secret ingredient in every successful sale.

A – Affirm. Great salespeople are also great listeners. They listen to understand, not to reply. They affirm their customers' needs, concerns, and aspirations. They make their customers feel seen, heard, and valued. Just like my mother always had cake ready for unexpected guests, great salespeople are always ready to greet their customers with a smile and a story.

K – Knowledge. But being a great salesperson isn't just about making connections and affirming customers; it's also about sharing knowledge. It's about educating customers, helping them understand their options, guiding them towards the best solution. It's about offering not just a product, but a learning experience.

E – Emotion. Finally, great salespeople know the power of emotion. They know that people don't buy products; they buy stories, experiences, feelings. They add a dash of emotion to every sales pitch, making their brand unforgettable. Just like a delicious piece of cake leaves a yummy in your tummy, so does an emotionally charged sales pitch.

Sales is not just about persuasion; it's about connecting, affirming, teaching, and most importantly, serving it up with a sprinkling of emotion. So, go ahead, serve your CAKE, and maybe a small slice of PIE too. After all, some consumers need a little nudge.

The Appetizer:

Mastering Your Nudge: The Key to Turning Prospects into Loyal Customers

The business landscape has drastically changed over the years, and traditional sales funnel models are no longer enough to convert prospects into loyal customers. These days, companies need to have a little nudge to make their brand stand out and get noticed. But what exactly is a nudge? It's the little push you give to get people excited about doing business with you. And it's crucial in changing prospects into leads, leads into customers, and turning customers into referral sources.

What makes a good nudge, and how you can use it to turn your prospects into loyal customers. We'll look at the different ways you can get in front of people and the importance of answering their objections and reinforcing their buying factors.

Understanding the Importance of a Good Nudge:

A nudge is more than just a sales tactic. It's the art of persuasion, and it's essential to build a loyal customer base. The key is to create a connection with your prospects and build trust. A good nudge should be tailored to your target audience, and it should quickly grab their attention. It should make them feel like they need your product or service and that you're the best option to provide it.

Ways to Get in Front of People:

In today's digital age, there are multiple ways to get in front of people. Social media, Google My Business, email marketing, videos, and testimonials are just a few of the options at your disposal. Your Business Coach will help you sort your way through this jungle of options. However, just getting in front of people is not enough. You need to deliver content that resonates with them, provides value, and convinces them to act.

Answering the Five Objections:

Every prospect has their objections, and it's your job to address them before they become a barrier to purchase. By addressing these objections through your marketing and sales strategy, you can remove any barriers and make it easier for your prospects to say, "Yes." For example, if price is a common objection, you could offer a discount or payment plan to make your product or service more affordable.

Reinforcing the Seven Buying Factors:

In addition to addressing objections, you also need to reinforce the seven buying factors that influence a customer's decision to purchase. By highlighting these factors, you can showcase the unique value proposition of your brand and create a sense of urgency among your prospects.

Closing the Sale:

Finally, it's time to close the sale. This is where your nudge comes into play. A good nudge should create a sense of urgency and motivate your prospects to act. You could offer a limited-time discount or free trial to encourage them to make a purchase. Remember, the goal is to turn prospects into loyal customers, and the best way to do that is by creating a positive buying experience.

Mastering your nudge is the key to turning prospects into loyal customers. By understanding the importance of a good nudge, leveraging different ways to get in front of people, addressing objections, reinforcing buying factors, and closing the sale, you can build a successful business. Keep in mind that the sales process is constantly evolving, and it's essential to stay adaptable and innovative to succeed. With the right nudge, you can turn prospects into loyal customers and create a thriving business that stands out in a crowded market.

The Buffet

The Power of Storytelling in Business

The power of storytelling in business! It's like a captivating novel that pulls you right into its pages, making you feel every emotion, every triumph, every challenge. It's not just about telling tales; it's about weaving a narrative that speaks to the heart and soul of those who hear it.

The BACON of storytelling in business! Let's break it down:

B - Bonding: Just like a good book that draws you in, storytelling in business is about creating an emotional connection with your audience. It's not just about telling tales; it's about weaving a narrative that resonates with the heart and soul of those who hear it.

Start by identifying the emotional core of your business. What are the values that drive you? What is the passion that fuels your work? This is the heart of your story, the ingredient that will help your audience form an emotional bond with your business. Share your journey, your struggles, your victories, and your dreams. Make it personal, make it real, make it something that your audience can connect with on a deep level.

A - Arousal of Emotions: Storytelling is our oldest form of communication, our way to share experiences and teach lessons. In business, it stimulates emotions and energy, engaging, inspiring, and motivating your audience in ways that numbers and data can't.

Stir up emotions with your story. Great stories aren't just informative; they are also emotionally engaging. Use vivid descriptions, powerful metaphors, and compelling anecdotes to make your audience feel what you felt, to experience your journey as if it were their own. Make them laugh, make them cry, make them feel inspired and motivated. The more you arouse their emotions, the more memorable your story will be.

C - Connection: Imagine yourself as a customer, faced with a choice between two products. One tells you what it does, the other tells you a story - a story of passion, effort, and impact. Which one would you choose? The one with the story, right? That's because stories connect us, transforming your business from a faceless entity into a living, breathing character.

Build a strong connection with your audience by making your story relatable. Show them that you understand their needs, their desires, their challenges. Show them how your business can help them achieve their goals, solve their problems, make their lives better. The stronger the connection, the more likely your audience is to trust you, to believe in your story, and to become loyal customers.

O - Objective: The purpose of business stories isn't just to entertain but to deliver a specific message, an objective, and ultimately, a desired outcome. When you craft an exciting and consistent story that explains why your company is unique, it helps you stand out from the competition. What are you trying to achieve with your story? Do you want to inspire your audience? Do you want to educate them? Do you want to persuade them to buy your product or service? Be clear about your objective and make sure every part of your story supports it.

N - Noteworthy: Stories are memorable. They linger in the minds and hearts of those who hear them, long after the numbers have been forgotten. So, remember, stories engage. Stories inspire. Stories sell. And most importantly, stories remain. That's the noteworthy power of storytelling.

So, make your story memorable. Use catchy phrases, powerful quotes, surprising twists, and inspiring endings to make your story stick in your audience's minds. Remember, people may forget what you said or did, but they will never forget how you made them feel.

When working on your story, remember Bonding, Arousal of emotions, Connection, Objective, and make it Noteworthy. Now, isn't that a delicious recipe for success? So, go ahead and cook up your BACON narrative. It might take some time and effort, but when you see your audience savoring your story, hanging onto your every word, and coming back for more, you'll know it was all worth it. After all, who can resist a great big serving of BACON?

Sharing Your Story - Platforms and Strategies

Choosing the right platforms for advertising can seem overwhelming, but it really boils down to understanding your target audience and goals. Sharing your business story is like opening a captivating book to the world, and choosing the right platforms and strategies is crucial to ensure your story reaches as many readers as possible.

Understand Your Audience

Who are they? Where do they spend their time online? What kind of content do they consume? Understanding your customer's online behavior is essential. For example, if they're mostly young adults, platforms like Instagram might be more suitable. If they're professionals, consider LinkedIn or business blogs.

Refer to Creating a Customer Avatar in this Chapter.

Define Your Goals

Are you trying to boost brand awareness, generate leads, or drive sales? Different platforms serve different purposes. Social media can be great for building brand awareness, while email marketing might be a better choice for lead generation and nurturing.

Evaluate Each Platform

Website: Your website is your digital storefront where customers learn about your business. It's crucial for all businesses. It's an excellent place to share your story in a format that reflects your brand. Use compelling images, videos, and text to tell your story in a way that engages visitors.

Blog: A blog provides a more informal platform to share deeper insights into your journey, values, and vision. It's a perfect place to offer behind-the-scenes glimpses, success stories, and thought leadership pieces. Blogs can help establish your business as an industry expert, improve SEO, and provide value to your audience. It's great if you have the capacity to create regular, valuable content.

Social Media: Platforms like Facebook, Instagram, LinkedIn, and Twitter offer opportunities to share different aspects of your story with diverse audiences. They can help increase visibility, engage with your audience, and even sell directly. Use captivating visuals, hashtags, and appealing captions to draw people in. Talk to your Business Coach to determine where you should be posting and where you should be passing.

Podcasts and Webinars: Sharing your story in audio or video format can be a powerful way to connect with your audience. If your audience consumes audio content and your subject matter lends itself well to conversation or interviews, this could be a great option for you. People can hear your passion and see your authenticity, making your story even more relatable.

Email Newsletters: Email marketing allows for direct, personalized communication with your audience. It's effective for nurturing leads and retaining customers. Regular updates to your subscribers can include elements of your story, keeping your audience engaged and fostering a sense of community.

Test and Measure

Trial and error is part of the process. Start small, measure the results, and adjust your strategy accordingly. Use analytics to see which platforms are driving results.

Consider Your Resources

Do you have the time, skills, and budget to maintain a consistent presence on the chosen platforms? It's better to do one or two platforms well than spreading yourself too thin. Coaches and Contractors should be leaned on to get these tasks done right.

In the end, the right mix will depend on your specific business, audience, and goals. You might need to experiment a bit before finding the most effective approach. Just remember, digital marketing is a marathon, not a sprint. Patience and persistence are key.

Keep in Mind

Consistency: Ensure your story is consistent across all platforms. This doesn't necessarily mean you should or have to share the same content everywhere; if you can, tailor your message to each platform, when necessary, while maintaining a consistent brand voice and narrative.

Engagement: Encourage interaction by asking questions, soliciting feedback, and responding to comments. This two-way communication can make your audience feel part of your story.

Visual Storytelling: Use images, infographics, and videos to convey your story. Visuals can evoke emotions and make your story more memorable.

Collaborations: Partner with influencers or other businesses that align with your values. Their audience can become part of your narrative, expanding your reach.

Authenticity: Be real and transparent. Authenticity resonates with audiences and builds trust.

Remember, your business story is not just what you've done or what you sell; it's who you are, why you do what you do, and how you make a difference. So, go ahead, open that book, and let the world read your unique business story.

Cause Marketing: What It Is & How to Do It

Cause marketing is like a heartwarming partnership between a business and a nonprofit for mutual benefit. It's not just about making a profit; it's about making a difference. It's about aligning your business with a cause that resonates with your values, your mission, and your audience.

You might be wondering, "Why cause marketing?" Well, cause marketing is a powerful way to show your customers that you care about more than just the bottom line. It helps you build a positive brand image, strengthen customer loyalty, and make a meaningful impact on a cause you believe in. In fact, according to a Cone Communications study, 91% of global consumers expect companies to do more than make a profit; they should also operate responsibly to address social and environmental issues.

So, how do you do cause marketing? Here are some steps to guide you:

1. **Choose a Cause:** The first step is to choose a cause that aligns with your business values and mission. It should be something you genuinely care about and something your audience can relate to.
2. **Find a Partner:** Once you've chosen a cause, look for a nonprofit organization that works in that area. Make sure you do your research and choose an organization that is reputable and transparent about how they use their funds.
3. **Develop a Campaign:** Work with your nonprofit partner to develop a campaign. This could involve donating a portion of your sales to the cause, sponsoring an event, or launching a co-branded product. Be creative and think about how you can make the biggest impact.
4. **Promote Your Campaign:** Use your marketing channels to promote your campaign. Tell your audience about your partnership, your goals, and how they can get involved. Remember, storytelling is key here. Make your audience feel part of your journey and your mission.
5. **Measure Impact:** Finally, don't forget to measure the impact of your campaign. This could involve tracking sales, social media engagement, or the amount of money raised for the cause. Share these results with your audience to show them the difference their support has made.

Remember, cause marketing is not just a marketing strategy; it's a commitment to making a positive impact on the world. So go ahead, find a cause you believe in, and start making a difference today. Who knows, you might just find that the greatest benefit of cause marketing is not the profit you make, but the change you create.

Community Involvement: Why It Matters and How to Get Involved

Oh, the magic of community involvement for small businesses! It's like a warm embrace that says, "We're here with you, for you." But why does it matter, and how can you, as a small business owner, get involved?

Community involvement is not just about doing good; it's about being a good neighbor. It's about understanding that your business is part of a larger ecosystem, that your success is tied to the health and prosperity of your community.

Why does it matter? Well, community involvement helps build strong relationships with customers, increases brand visibility, and creates a positive reputation. It shows your customers that you care about more than just profits; you care about people. And in today's socially conscious world, that matters a lot.

According to a study by Cone Communications, 87% of consumers said they would purchase a product because a company advocated for an issue they cared about. That's the power of community involvement!

So, how can you get involved? Here are some ways:

1. **Sponsor Local Events:** Whether it's a local fair, charity run, or school event, sponsoring local events is a great way to show your support for the community while also increasing your brand visibility.
2. **Volunteer:** Encourage your team to volunteer for local causes. This could involve cleaning up a park, serving food at a homeless shelter, or mentoring local students. Not only will this make a positive impact on your community, but it will also boost employee morale and team spirit.
3. **Donate:** Consider donating a portion of your profits to a local charity. Or you could set up a donation box in your store or on your website.

4. **Partner with Local Businesses:** Collaborate with other local businesses on joint initiatives or events. This can help strengthen your local business community and provide mutual benefits.

5. **Offer Free Workshops or Classes:** Share your expertise with the community by offering free workshops or classes. This can help position your business as a leader in your field while also providing value to your community.

Remember, community involvement is not a one-time thing; it's a long-term commitment. But the rewards - stronger customer relationships, increased brand loyalty, and a more vibrant community - are well worth the effort. So go ahead, roll up your sleeves, and start making a difference in your community today. After all, isn't that what being a good neighbor is all about?

Time to Oink!

Organize, Internalize, and Nurture the Knowledge!

Creating a meaningful business narrative is like crafting a compelling story. It's an art that requires imagination, authenticity, and a deep understanding of your audience. Here are some steps to help you create a business narrative that resonates:

1. **Define Your Core Values:** Just as every character in a story has their beliefs and values, so does your business. What do you stand for? What drives your decisions and actions? Defining your core values is the first step in creating your business narrative.

2. **Identify Your Unique Selling Proposition (Your WIN):** What makes your business unique? Why should customers choose you over your competitors? Identifying your WIN helps you stand out from the crowd and gives your audience a reason to care about your story.

3. **Know Your Audience:** A good storyteller knows their audience. Who are you trying to reach with your narrative? What are their needs, preferences, and pain points? Understanding your audience helps you craft a narrative that resonates with them.

4. **Share Your Journey:** Every story has a beginning, middle, and end. Share your journey – how you started, the challenges you faced, the victories you achieved, and where you're headed. This not only makes your narrative engaging but also relatable.

5. **Be Authentic:** Authenticity is key in storytelling. Be honest, be transparent, be real. Authentic narratives build trust and foster strong relationships with your audience.

6. **Use Emotional Appeal:** Stories that evoke emotions are more memorable. Whether it's joy, surprise, or inspiration, use emotional appeal to connect with your audience on a deeper level.

7. **Incorporate Storytelling Techniques:** Use techniques like metaphors, anecdotes, and vivid descriptions to make your narrative more engaging and memorable.

8. **Keep It Simple and Clear:** A good story is easy to understand. Keep your narrative simple, clear, and focused. Avoid jargon and complicated language.
9. **Involve Your Audience:** Make your audience part of your story. Ask for their feedback, share their success stories, and celebrate their achievements. This not only makes your narrative more engaging but also builds a sense of community.
10. **Evolve Your Story:** As your business grows and evolves, so should your narrative. Keep it updated and relevant to reflect your current reality and future aspirations.

Remember, a good business narrative is not just about telling people what you do; it's about showing them why it matters. So, go ahead, pick up your pen, and start crafting your business narrative today. After all, every business has a story to tell. What's yours?

Activity #1 - Your Customer Avatars

A Customer Avatar, also known as a Buyer Persona, is an essential tool in the world of marketing and sales. But why exactly do you need one?

Picture this: You're at a crowded party, trying to get someone's attention. You could shout out random names, hoping that someone would turn around. Or, you could know their name, their likes, dislikes, interests - and strike up a conversation that would instantly draw them in.

That's what a Customer Avatar does for your business.

It's a detailed profile of your ideal customers - their demographics, psychographics, behaviors, and needs. It gives you a clear picture of who you're talking to when you create marketing messages or develop products.

Having a Customer Avatar means you're not shooting in the dark. You're not wasting time and money on messages that don't resonate. Instead, you're speaking directly to the people who are most likely to be interested in what you have to offer.

In essence, a Customer Avatar allows you to personalize your approach, making your marketing more effective and your products more appealing. It helps you understand your customers' pain points, desires, and motivations so you can offer solutions that truly meet their needs.

So, do you need a Customer Avatar? If you want to connect with your audience, save resources, and drive your business success, the answer is a resounding yes!

Creating a Customer Avatar

Download the Customer Avatar worksheet, available at the end of this chapter, and start defining your individual customers.

Demographics - Knowing who your customers are is essential to creating effective marketing messages and products. Demographics include basic information such as age, gender, location, and income. By understanding these details, you can tailor your marketing messages to your ideal customer and make them more relevant.

Psychographics - Psychographics go beyond demographics and describe your customer's values, beliefs, and goals. Understanding what motivates your customers can help you create messaging that resonates with them on a deeper level. Ask yourself: What are your customer's biggest motivators? What are their biggest fears and aspirations? Knowing these details can inform your messaging and product development.

Knowledge - Understanding how your customers learn can also help you create compelling marketing messages. Some customers may prefer visual content, while others may prefer written content. Some customers may be more likely to learn through video tutorials, while others may prefer podcasts. By understanding how your customers absorb information, you can create the right type of content that speaks to them in a way they understand.

Pain Points - Knowing your customer's pain points is essential to creating messaging that resonates and encourages them to act. Pain Points can be anything from a problem they are facing to a feeling of frustration or lack of fulfilment in their life. By addressing these Pain Points, you can create messaging that speaks to your customer's needs and encourages them to act.

Objections - Finally, it's essential to address your customer's objections to your product or service. This could be pricing concerns, a lack of trust in the brand, or a perceived lack of value. By addressing these objections head-on, you can create messaging that helps to alleviate these concerns and encourages your customers to engage.

Creating a customer avatar is an essential tool for any marketer looking to create effective marketing messages and successful products. By understanding demographics, psychographics, knowledge, pain points, and objections, you can create messaging that speaks directly to your ideal customer and encourages them to act. Take the time to create customer avatars for each of your different customers, and you'll see a dramatic improvement in the effectiveness of your marketing messages and the success of your products.

Activity #2 – Sales Bingo

There are 5 basic Objections for NOT buying your product or service (No Trust, No Value, No Urgency, No Desire, and No Need) and 5 strong Emotional Triggers that people act upon (Greed, Pride, Envy, Fear, and Shame). Download the Sales Bingo Worksheet at the end of this chapter, to see if you can create compelling reasons, in each of these 25 squares, to get your potential customers to overcome their objection while sparking an emotional trigger that will get them to purchase your product or service. Be careful when addressing Shame, Envy, and Greed. You want to nudge your customers not alienate them.

Here are some general statements to get you thinking. Use them as a starting off point to write your own sales message that aligns with your specific product or service.

- No Trust vs. Greed: "We've helped hundreds of customers save money with our product. You can check their testimonials on our website."
- No Trust vs. Pride: "Our premium service is trusted by industry leaders. Join the elite group of satisfied customers."
- No Trust vs. Envy: "See how our clients are outperforming their competitors after using our product?"
- No Trust vs. Fear: "Without a reliable product like ours, you risk falling behind. Don't let that happen."
- No Trust vs. Shame: "You don't want to be the last one to adapt to new innovations. Trust us to keep up with trends."

- No Value vs. Greed: "Our product offers great value for money, helping you get more for less."
- No Value vs. Pride: "Investing in our high-quality product is a sign of your commitment to excellence."
- No Value vs. Envy: "Our customers are enjoying unprecedented growth. Don't you want the same?"
- No Value vs. Fear: "Without our valuable solution, you could miss key opportunities."
- No Value vs. Shame: "Don't settle for less when you can have the best."

- No Urgency vs. Greed: "Act now to secure our product at a limited-time discounted price."
- No Urgency vs. Pride: "Be the first to benefit from our latest update."
- No Urgency vs. Envy: "Your competitors are already taking advantage of our offer. Don't get left behind."
- No Urgency vs. Fear: "Delaying might cost you more in the long run."
- No Urgency vs. Shame: "Don't miss out on what others are already benefiting from."

- No Desire vs. Greed: "Our product can help you achieve your goals faster and more efficiently."
- No Desire vs. Pride: "Owning our product is an achievement in itself."
- No Desire vs. Envy: "Imagine the success others are experiencing with our product. You can have it too."
- No Desire vs. Fear: "Without our product, you're missing out on key benefits."
- No Desire vs. Shame: "Don't miss out on the opportunity to improve your status with our product."

- No Need vs. Greed: "Even if you don't need our product now, it is a great investment for future gains."
- No Need vs. Pride: "Our product is an essential tool for those who aspire to be the best."
- No Need vs. Envy: "Others are leveraging our product to surpass their peers. What about you?"
- No Need vs. Fear: "You might not need our product now, but are you prepared for future challenges?"
- No Need vs. Shame: "Stay ahead of the curve; don't be the only one without our proven solution."

Activity #3 – Purchasing FACTORS

Download the Purchasing FACTORS Worksheet, at the end of this chapter, to effectively establish motivational strategies that drive customers to purchase your products or services.

There are 7 essential reasons why customers choose to buy from you: Fondness - they genuinely like you, Authority - you are recognized as a credible expert, Consistency - people gravitate towards what they are accustomed to buying, Testimonials - customers feel more confident when purchasing products endorsed by others, Obsession - certain products become indispensable to customers, Reciprocity - individuals prefer buying from those who have supported them, and Scarcity - customers are more likely to make a purchase if they fear missing out.

Craft two compelling messages for each Purchasing Factor - one to promote the overall industry, for those who don't understand the need for your product or service, and another to substantiate why your specific product is unparalleled within that industry.

Activity #4 – Features, Benefits, and SIZZLE!

There is too much direct and indirect competition out there. You cannot rely on just telling the world what you do and how it helps them fulfill their needs and wants. You must make them feel something. You must create a deep desire that only your product or service can fill. And that feeling must linger long after the sale.

1. Features tell the world what you do.
2. Benefits explain the logical reason for doing business with you.
3. SIZZLE justifies the purchase at a deep emotional level, it gets them to sign on the dotted line, and entices them to send referrals your way.

Download the "Features, Benefits, and SIZZLE" Worksheet at the end of this chapter and write down how your competition goes to market in each of these three areas. Then explain why you have more impressive Features, Benefits, and SIZZLE!

Activity #5 – Huh, Hmm, Hey!

Are you getting your customers potential customers to go through the "Huh – Hmm - Hey Cycle?"

They start out as **LEADS**. What are you doing to get noticed? How are you differentiating yourself, your solutions, and your brand? What are you doing to get them to say, "Huh, who are these guys?"

Once you get that nibble, they turn into **PROSPECTS**. It's time to set that hook with interest and desire. Court them with promises of unbelievable pleasure and alleviated pain. Your goal is to get them to say, "Hmm, let's try these guys."

Finally, don't just deliver...always overdeliver. Fulfil your promises and give them more than they expected. Treat your **CUSTOMERS** like family, cherish them, and give them more than your competition can offer. You want them saying, "HEY, I love these guys!"

This is how you create long-lasting, loyal customers that will go out of their way to bring you continued business, recommendations, and referrals.

Download the "Huh, Hmm, Hey!" Worksheet and uncover what your potential, loyal customers are needing, thinking, feeling, and doing about it in every stage of the Customer Journey?

"Huh, who are these guys? Hmm, maybe I'll try these guys. Hey, I love these guys!"
Get into their heads and hearts and then develop the plan.

Activity #6 – The Master Grid

Embark on a journey of strategic planning with the "The Master Grid" Worksheet. This brainstorming tool is your secret weapon to crafting Social Media Posts that effectively tap into your customers' key decision-making triggers.

The worksheet is divided into three strategic ROWS:

Value: This row helps you articulate the importance and necessity of your product, showcasing why it's more than just a good choice—it's a significant one.

Objections Beaters: Here, we tackle potential roadblocks head-on. This row guides you in crafting responses to possible objections, paving the way from a hesitant 'No' to a confident 'YES'.

Shareability: This row focuses on creating posts that catches the eye; makes people stand up and take notice. Posts that will inspire your audience to share and discuss your content.

The worksheet also features COLUMNS, representing the three primary decision-making processes of your customers:

Brain: This column focuses on logical decisions, helping you appeal to the rational side of your customers.

Heart: This column targets emotional decisions, guiding you in connecting with your customers on a deeper, more personal level.

Gut: This column caters to spontaneous decisions, enabling you to create content that prompts quick, instinctive actions from your customers.

Here are some sample statements to get you thinking. Use them as a jumping off point to write your own sales message that aligns with your specific product or service.

Value

Brain: Just like the King in chess, our product is the cornerstone of your strategy. It's crafted with precision, backed by data, and designed to deliver exceptional results. Why? Because you deserve nothing less.

Heart: Our product isn't just an item; it's a partner on your journey. It's there when you need it, offering support, comfort, and reliability. It's a companion that understands you and caters to your needs.

Gut: Sometimes, you just know. You feel it in your gut. That's how our product is - intuitive, easy-to-use, and instantly recognizable as a game-changer.

Objections Beaters

Brain: Doubts? Let's address them head-on. Our product isn't just a purchase; it's an investment, a promise of quality, and a commitment to constant innovation. Say YES to excellence.

Heart: Fear of change can be daunting. But remember, every great journey begins with a single step. Our product is that step towards a better tomorrow. Trust your heart, embrace the new.

Gut: Hesitation can be a hurdle, but it shouldn't stand in your way. Our product is designed for spontaneous decisions, for those who seize the moment and leap towards success.

Shareability

Brain: Our product is worth talking about. Its innovative features, superior quality, and excellent performance make it a topic of engaging and intelligent conversations.

Heart: Share the love, spread the joy. Our product brings people together, creates shared experiences, and builds lasting relationships. It's not just shareable; it's lovable.

Gut: Fun, exciting, and intriguing - that's our product for you. It's the kind of thing you can't wait to share, to show off, to celebrate.

Remember, every square on the chessboard matters, every move counts. Value, Objections Beaters, Shareability - they're all interconnected, all crucial pieces of the puzzle. Brain, Heart, Gut - they're not just decision-making tools; they're pathways to success.

So, are you ready to master the game? Ready to conquer the grid? Download "The Master Grid" Worksheet today and start your journey towards creating social media posts that hit all your customers' triggers.

Download the Worksheets

Worksheet: Customer Avatar
Worksheet: Sales Bingo
Worksheet: Purchasing FACTORS
Worksheet: Features, Benefits, and SIZZLE
Worksheet: The Master Grid

BLT

Begin Immediately, Learn Continuously, and Teach Others!

Embrace the power of your journey, the magic in your story, and the value in your experiences. Your business is not just an entity; it's a saga of passion, hard work, and resilience. It's a narrative that can inspire, motivate, and connect with your customers on a profound level.

Remember, storytelling isn't just about narrating events; it's about weaving a tapestry of experiences that resonate with your audience. It's about showing them the heart behind the brand and the soul within the product. Your story has the power to humanize your brand, to build trust, and to foster a deep sense of loyalty among your customers.

You are the GOAT - the Greatest of All Things - when it comes to your offering. You've walked the path, faced the challenges, celebrated the victories, and learned from the setbacks. You hold the ultimate knowledge, the unique insights, and the invaluable experiences that make your offering truly special.

Sharing your story may seem daunting at first, but remember, every great tale begins with a single word. And once you get started, you'll find that it flows as naturally as a river, cascading from one milestone to another, carrying your audience along on a journey they'll never forget. It will become as easy and fulfilling as enjoying a piece of cake!

So, stand tall at the helm of your narrative. Let your voice ring clear and true. Share your story with the world, for it's a story worth telling, a story worth hearing, a story that can change lives and shape destinies.

Take a deep breath, gather your thoughts, and let's get started. It's time to share your journey, your triumphs, your lessons, and your vision. It's time to show the world why you're the GOAT in your field.

Go ahead, ignite the spark of inspiration, fuel the fire of success, and light up the world with your story. You've got this!

Conclusion

Uncover YOUR 5 Sizzling Secrets of Business Success!

B - Beliefs, Values, Vision, and Mission: Think of these as the secret recipe for your grandma's famous pie - unique, heartwarming, and irresistible. They are the ingredients that give your small business its distinct flavor and identity. They guide your decisions, shape your culture, and attract customers who share your values. Without them, you're just another pie in the bakery.

A - Analytics and Processes: These are the unsung champions, akin to stage crew in a theatrical show. Operating behind the curtains, they ensure everything functions without a hitch. They assist you in assessing performance, optimizing operations, and making data-driven decisions. In their absence, your venture could descend into a dramatic disaster!

C - Your Crew, Contractors, Coaches, and Mentors: Employees, Contractors, Coaches, and Mentors: These are the shining stars of your business, much like the members of a hit band. Everyone brings a unique set of expertise, contributing to the symphony of success. Without them, there's no melody, only silence.

O - Preparing for Obstacles, and Objections: This is akin to possessing a map for a treasure hunt. It aids you in foreseeing hurdles, charting your path, and maintaining focus on the goal. Without foresight and preparation, your business expedition could end up astray, lost in the vast ocean!

N - Your Narrative, The Way You Tell Your Story: This is the blockbuster script of your business journey. It enthralls audiences, distinguishes you from rivals, and establishes an emotional bond with your customers. Without a riveting narrative, your business is like a movie devoid of a plot - unlikely to top the charts!

So, are you ready to turn up the heat and blaze a trail to success? Embrace these scorching secrets and watch your business sizzle!

Who is Marty Jalove?

Happiness Instigator, Communication Coach, and Master of Human Connection

From the moment Marty Jalove chooses to step on a stage, walk into a boardroom, or simply interact with others, one thing becomes abundantly clear: Marty is on a mission to help the world discover the secrets to happiness, success, and fulfillment. With a unique blend of charisma, expertise, and personal experience, Marty has made it his life's work to create powerful connections, inspire change, and unlock the potential in others.

"Shine, Sharpen, and Share!"
Marty Jalove, Master Happiness

Master Happiness
Business Success Coach

Are you a small business feeling lost in the hustle and bustle of everyday life? Stagnant sales, apathetic employees, or a crumbling customer base?

Marty Jalove wants to help your company identify and amplify your core values, vision, and mission. Let's use this manual as a playbook for the next chapter in your business's success story.

Marty will help you and your team find focus, feel fulfilled and have fun. He will help you set goals, create a plan, and realize dreams!

Book an appointment with Marty now for a free consultation on how he can best help you reach and exceed your business goals!

You'll be glad that you did.

www.MasterHappiness.com

Master Happiness
Sizzling Keynote Speaker

Are you looking for a keynote speaker who will truly inspire your audience?

Meet Marty Jalove of Master Happiness – an extraordinary motivational speaker with stories of success and failure, thoughtful advice on how to find fulfillment, and the ability to make any event lighthearted yet meaningful. With his expertise in focus, fulfillment and fun, he'll provide your team or event empowering strategies that they may never have considered before!

Marty's powerful presentations not only energize attendees but also offer them a unique path towards mastering happiness at work, in relationships, and in their lives overall. And his wit-filled humor is sure to leave everyone smiling after the session ends.

Don't wait - book Marty Jalove from Master Happiness now before someone else does! Scan here to get started.

www.MasterHappiness.com

Check out
Bacon Bits with Master Happiness
wherever you listen to podcasts!

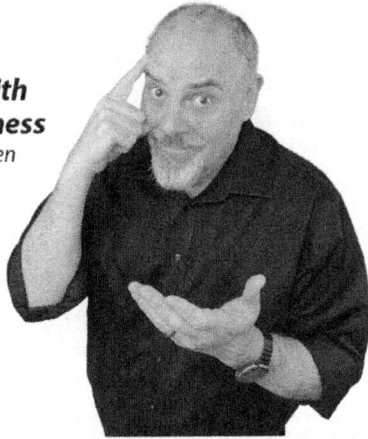

Master Happiness
Executive, Career, & Life Coach

Are you looking for more out of life but feel stuck in the same rut?

Master Happiness Executive, Career and Life Coach can help you uncover what's been hidden in front of you all along. You will gain access to powerful tools that will let you peel back the layers holding your true passions hostage. Get in touch with your Inner Bacon and get ready to take control of your life!

Take advantage of our expertise and experience as we guide you on a process total transformation. Your career-life balance can finally be restored - giving renewed purpose, flexibility, stability, and appreciation like never before! With enhanced communication skills comes empowerment enabling better relationships with yourself and those around you. What are you waiting for?!

Book an appointment with us now so we can start reclaiming YOUR future from today!

www.MasterHappiness.com

Master Happiness
Team Building

Do you need help boosting communication and teamwork within your organization?

Our team-building workshops are the perfect way to take a break from the monotony of everyday life, learn how to think on your feet, and break out of comfort zones. Improv training teaches you how to say "Yes, and" which encourages collaboration between colleagues in order to create innovative new ideas.

With our Improv training workshops, you will be able to not only show recognition for what others have said but also enhance their ideas with your own thoughts. So why wait? Let's create a customized team-building workshops for your team and get the most out of every workday!

Learn more TODAY—and get a happier workplace in your tomorrow!

www.MasterHappiness.com

Made in the USA
Monee, IL
17 August 2023